Grade 3

Gifted & Talented™

Reading, Writing & Math

Cover Illustration by Mark Stephens
Written by Tracy Masonis and Vicky Shiotsu

Dear Parents,

Gifted & Talented Reading, Writing & Math has been designed specifically to promote development of analytic thinking, language arts, and math skills. The activities in this book use a variety of critical strategies, including activities to spark your child's imagination, encourage brainstorming, and sharpen math skills.

The activities are intended to help develop reading, writing, and math skills that your child will use at school and home. Most of the activities can be completed directly on the workbook pages. In some instances, though, your child might like to use a separate sheet of paper to interpret what has been read or work out math problems.

While working in this book, your child may be inspired to create his or her own story or math problems. If so, have your child present his or her work and explain the strategies to you. Praise your child's efforts, and encourage him or her to continue creating them. This type of activity not only stimulates creativity and independent thinking, but also deepens your child's love of learning.

Flash Kids
A Division of Barnes & Noble
122 Fifth Avenue
New York, NY 10011

ISBN: 978-1-4114-9555-5

Please submit all inquiries to FlashKids@bn.com

Printed and bound in China

10 9 8 7

Table of Contents—Reading

Knowing the Words/Vocabulary/Language Development

Elements of Stories

Reading Comprehension

Table of Contents—Writing

Writing Words

Writing Sentences

Sentence Starters

Writing Stories

The Senses

Setting-Place

More Stories

Just for Fun

Writing Answer Key

Table of Contents—Math

Number Sense

Operations and Computation

Patterns

Money

Fractions

Logical Thinking

Measurement

Geometry

Statistics and Probability

Math Answer Key

Circle a Synonym!

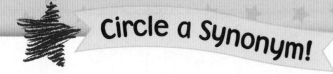

Words that mean the **same** thing, or almost the same thing, are called **synonyms**.

Circle a synonym for the **boldfaced** word in each line. Then select another synonym from the Word List to write in the blanks.

Word List		
silky	lively	prickly
slender	sturdy	fatigued

1. **sharp:**   pointed   spear   _____

2. **strong:**   gym   tough   _____

3. **smooth:**   velvety   chocolate   _____

4. **narrow:**   bridge   thin   _____

5. **frisky:**   playful   haughty   _____

6. **exhausted:**   naughty   tired   _____

Selecting Synonyms

Select three synonyms to match the **boldfaced** word in each row. Circle your choices.

1. **frighten:**   terrify   scare   simple   horrify

2. **delicious:** scrumptious   yummy   ugly   tasty

3. **last:**   final   neat   end   ultimate

4. **trip:**   plane   journey   expedition   voyage

5. **neat:**   clean   tidy   new   orderly

Look at each picture below. Use the words you circled to write a list of synonyms to describe each picture.

Synonym Snob!

Sydney is a synonym snob! She hates to use the same words as everybody else. Help Sydney say her student council speech using super synonyms! Change each underlined word to a more exciting synonym. You may use the Word List below for ideas.

Word List

brainy	balmy	incredibly	bright
good	luminous	outrageously	kind
morning	superb	hello	polite
attend	fantastic	clever	elect
humid	hot	intelligent	orderly
pleasant	extremely	prepared	wonderful

Hi, my name is Sydney. I go to Aloha School in warm and sunny Hawaii. I would like to be on student council because I can do a great job. I am very smart, and I work hard. Also, I am very organized and nice to people. Those are the reasons you should vote for me!

Write Sydney's new speech on the lines below:

_____

_____

_____

_____

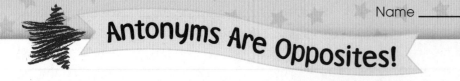

Antonyms Are Opposites!

Words with **opposite** meanings are called **antonyms**. Circle the pair of antonyms in each box. Complete each sentence with one of the circled words.

clean	shine	sparkle	dirty

Taking out the garbage made my hands _____.

After I take a bath, I feel very _____.

loving	gentle	loud	rough

My new cat was very _____ with her kittens.

The monkeys are _____ with each other when they play.

polite	chatty	horrible	rude

Shouting out in class is very _____.

The student was very _____ to her teacher.

tall	mean	kind	kite

The _____ boy had no friends.

A _____ friend is a nice friend to have.

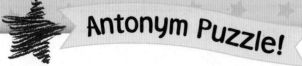

Antonym Puzzle!

Fill in the crossword puzzle below. Use the clues in the Word List, except choose each word's **opposite** meaning. Good Luck!

Word List

Across	Down
1. above	2. win
4. full	3. laugh
6. messy	5. war
8. easy	7. loose
9. serious	8. wet

Antonym Art

Antonyms are words that have **opposite** meanings. Draw an antonym for each word below.

beautiful

cheerful

serious

repair

smooth

enemy

gigantic

deserted

cruel

Different Meanings

Some words have more than one meaning.

The word *chicken* has more than one meaning. Look at the words below and their two meanings.

Below each picture, write the number that has the correct meaning.

bank: 1) a pile or heap
2) a container for saving money

box: 3) a container, usually with four sides
4) to fight with fists

fast: 5) quick, rapid, swift
6) to go without food

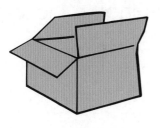

_____   _____   _____

_____   _____   _____

What Do You Mean?

Some words have more than one meaning. Look at the list below. Two different meanings are given for each word.

A   **B**

fit: healthy   the way something has the right size or shape

saw: looked   a tool or machine for cutting

yard: a unit of length   a piece of ground near a building

log: a daily record   a section of a tree

fire: to dismiss from   the flame, heat, and light caused by burning

Choose which meaning the **boldfaced** word has in each sentence below. Fill in the A or B circle. Then write the meaning on the line.

Ⓐ Ⓑ The gym teacher was very **fit**. _____

Ⓐ Ⓑ The Goodmans have a beautiful **yard**. _____

Ⓐ Ⓑ May I borrow your **saw** to cut this? _____

Ⓐ Ⓑ The principal needs to **fire** the lazy instructor. _____

Ⓐ Ⓑ I kept a **log** the entire time I was on the ship. _____

Ⓐ Ⓑ The **log** fell across the road during the storm. _____

Match That Meaning!

Read these different meanings for the word *key*.

key:

1) a small instrument for locking and unlocking things

3) one of a set of levers pressed down by the fingers in playing piano

2) a sheet or book of answers

4) a low island reef

Write the number of the correct meaning in each blank.

1. One piano _____ was stuck and I could not play that note.

2. My teacher read the corrections from the answer _____.

3. The Florida _____(s) are a very popular winter vacation choice.

4. This _____ will unlock the back door.

Bonus

5. My family went down to the Florida _____(s) for the summer. We brought the house _____, opened up the cottage, and unpacked. I love to play the piano on vacation, but the _____(s) always stick because it is so humid.

Common Corrections!

Some words look and sound very much alike, but have very different meanings. Look at the words and meanings below. Write the correct word to complete each sentence.

thorough: complete

through: in one side and out the other

then: at that time

than: a comparison

mere: a tiny bit

mirror: a reflective surface

I am taller _____ you by five inches!

Please do a _____ job when you sweep the floor.

There was a _____ drop of ketchup left in the bottle!

The ball went _____ the glass window!

Do your homework and _____ we will go play.

Do you have a _____ I could use?

Common Corrections!

Some words look and sound very much alike, but have very different meanings. Fill in the sentences below using the correct word.

Word List		
united	whether	now
untied	weather	know

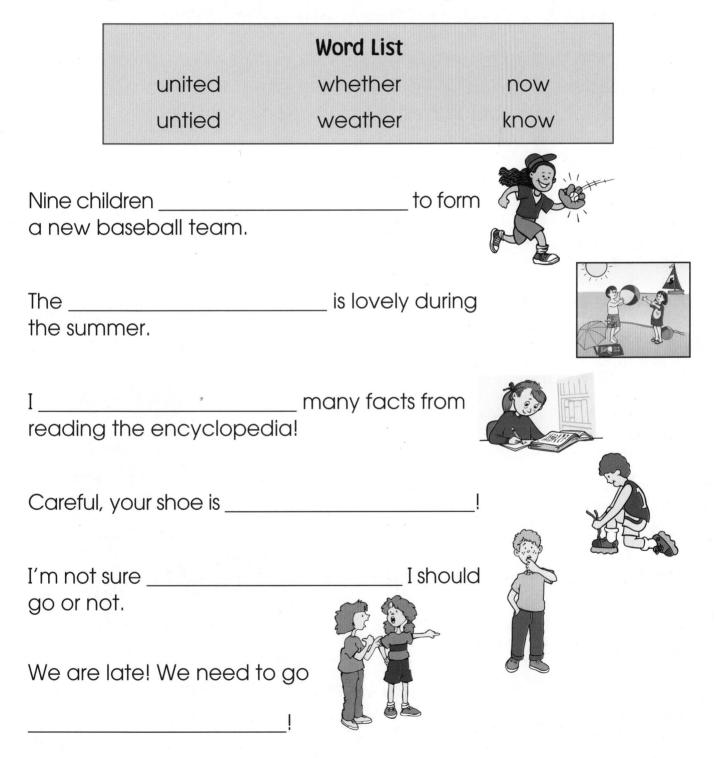

Nine children _____ to form a new baseball team.

The _____ is lovely during the summer.

I _____ many facts from reading the encyclopedia!

Careful, your shoe is _____!

I'm not sure _____ I should go or not.

We are late! We need to go _____!

Carmen's Context Clues!

Name _____

When you read, it's important to know about context clues. **Context clues** can help you to figure out the meaning of a word, or a missing word, just by looking at the **other words** in the sentence.

Read each sentence below. Circle the context clues, or other words in the sentence that give you hints. Choose a word from the Word List to replace the **boldfaced** word. Write it on the line.

Word List

real	tired	dry
dull	leave	

If a fire alarm goes off in my school, we **evacuate** the building. _____

I felt very **weary** after the ten-mile hike up the mountain. _____

Please use a **blunt** knife when you are carving wood. I don't want you to get hurt.

_____

The desert has a very **arid** climate.

_____

It is hard to believe the gigantic diamond is **genuine**. It is so large that it looks fake!

_____

What Do You Mean?

Choose a word from the Word List to replace the **boldfaced** word in each sentence. Write the word on the line. Use a dictionary to help you with new words.

Word List		
slow	thick	strict
serious	heavy	bright

The **dazzling** lights of Broadway made me want to be a star! _____

It was almost impossible to walk through the **dense** jungle leaves. _____

The **stout** old woman could hardly fit in the chair. I thought it might break! _____

The situation was **grave** when my little sister got lost in the huge mall. _____

The **sluggish** turtle walked two feet all day!

_____

The courtroom rules for silence are quite **severe**.

_____

Michelangelo the Magnificent!

Read the story and then use the context clues to answer the questions below.

There once lived a **magnificent** artist named Michelangelo. He was one of the world's greatest artists. He was born in Florence, Italy, in the year 1475. Michelangelo had **numerous** talents. He could paint, sculpt, and even write poetry.

Michelangelo is most **celebrated** for painting the Sistine Chapel ceiling. Thousands of tourists **flock** to see the ceiling each year. Visitors are usually amazed at the beautiful orange, red, and yellow paints he used. Michelangelo painted the ceiling in the most **vivid** colors.

Michelangelo could also take a crude block of marble and **transform** it into an extraordinary sculpture. He truly was magnificent!

Which **boldfaced** word in the story means…?

many _____

famous _____

gather _____

striking _____

change _____

outstanding _____

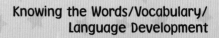

More Michelangelo!

Would you rather paint your room in a **vivid** color or a **dull** color? What color would you choose?

_____

Use **magnificent** in a sentence of your own:

_____

_____

What does the word **crude** mean?

_____

Draw a **crude** block of marble. Then draw a picture of what you would sculpt out of a block of marble.

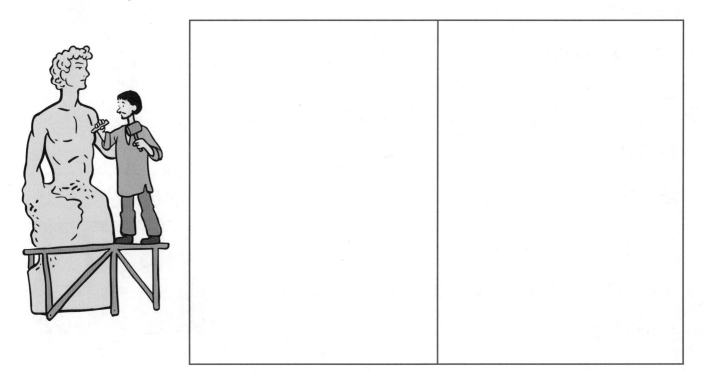

A Switch Is a Switch!

Choose the best meaning for the **boldfaced** word as it is used in the sentence. Circle your choice.

Mrs. Mitchell is so **trim**! I think it's because she is an aerobics instructor and stays in great shape.

A)   to cut

B)   to decorate

C)   slim

"Please, don't **hunch** over when you eat, Bill. Sitting like that is bad for your back, not to mention that it's also bad manners," said Bill's mom.

A)   a sudden idea, an intuitive feeling

B)   to push or thrust forward

C)   to bend into a hump

"I've got to **dash** inside the store. I'll only be a minute," I said to Barney.

A)   to break or smash

B)   to run quickly

C)   a small amount of an ingredient

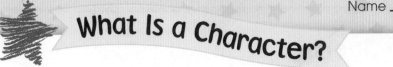

What Is a Character?

A **character** is the **person**, **animal**, or **object** that a story is about. You can't have a story without a character.

Characters are usually people, but sometimes they can be animals, aliens (!), or even objects that come to life. You can have many characters in a story.

Read the story below, and then answer the questions about character on the next page.

Rorie the Reader!

Rorie loved to read. Rorie would read everything she could find: books, magazines, even cereal boxes! She loved to read so much that she would always carry books in her bag in case she had a free second to read.

Rorie had blond hair and was very pale. Her mom would say, "Rorie, please go outside and play. You need to get some sunshine."

Rorie would answer, "Do I have to, Mom? I would rather read."

One day, Rorie's teacher said to her mom, "I have never seen a girl that loves to read so much. You are very lucky to have a daughter like Rorie." From then on, Rorie's mom let her read whenever she wanted.

Character Continued

First, authors must decide who their main character is going to be. Next, they decide what their main character looks like. Then, they reveal the character's personality by:

what the character does
what the character says
what other people say about the character

Who is the main character in "Rorie the Reader!"?

_____

What does Rorie look like? Describe her appearance on the line below:

_____

Give two examples of what Rorie **does** that shows that she loves to read:

Example 1) _____

Example 2) _____

Give an example of what Rorie **says** that reveals she loves to read:

_____

Give an example of what **other people say** about Rorie that shows she likes to read:

_____

Name _____

Character Interview—Lights! Camera! Action!

An **interview** occurs between two people, usually a reporter and another person. The interviewer asks questions for the person to answer.

Pretend that you are a reporter. Choose a character from a book that you have read. If you could ask the character anything you wanted to, what would you ask?

Make a **list of questions** you would like to ask your character:

1. _____

2. _____

3. _____

4. _____

Now pretend that your character has come to life and could **answer your questions**. Write what he, she, or it would say:

1. _____

2. _____

3. _____

4. _____

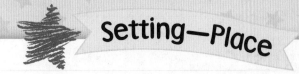

Setting—Place

Every story has a **setting**. The setting is the **place** where the story happens. Think of a place that you know well. It could be your room, your kitchen, your backyard, your classroom, or an imaginary place.

Brainstorm some words and ideas about that place. Think about what you see, hear, smell, taste, or feel in that place.

Brainstorm your ideas for a setting below:

_____

_____

_____

_____

see   hear   smell

taste   touch

_____

_____

_____

_____

_____

Where are we? _____

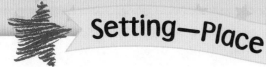

Setting—Place

Read the story below and answer the questions about the setting.

Italian Restaurant

My family lives over an Italian restaurant. The restaurant is on the bottom floor of the house, and we live on the second floor. There are always great smells coming from the restaurant kitchen, such as warm bread, boiling tomato sauce, and sweet chocolate cake. We also hear silverware clanking and lots of loud voices. Many people come in and out of the restaurant all day and night. The best part of living over the restaurant is that whenever we are hungry, we just go downstairs to eat!

What sounds would you hear living over the restaurant?

_____

What would you smell living over the restaurant?

_____

What would you see if you lived over the restaurant?

_____

Setting—Time

The **setting** is the **place** where the story happens. The setting is also the **time** in which the story happens. A reader needs to know **when** the story is happening. Does it take place at night? On a sunny day? In the future? During the winter?

Time can be: time of day
                 a holiday
                 a season of the year
                 a time in history
                 a time in the future

Read the following story. Then answer the questions below.

Pizza Night!

    Last Tuesday, we made pizzas for dinner. We made mini-pizzas out of pita bread, tomato sauce, mozzarella cheese, and vegetable toppings. Then my mom put our "M.P.s" (mini-pizzas) into the oven for the cheese to melt. Mmm-m-m! Delicious!

What time of day did this story take place? _____

What day of the week did this story take place? _____

What happened in the story?

_____

_____

_____

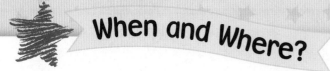

When and Where?

A **setting** tells **when** and **where** a story takes place. Read the story settings below. Describe when and where the story takes place.

Last winter, Michael's family went skiing in Stratton, Vermont. They spent a week skiing and sledding down the snowy slopes.

When did this story take place? _____

Where did this story take place? _____

Today we went to the Fourth of July Parade in West Hartford, Connecticut. All the Boy Scouts, Girl Scouts, and high school bands marched through the quaint town center.

When did this story take place? _____

Where did this story take place? _____

Living on the International Space Station for three months was not easy. The astronauts had to watch out for random asteroids and space debris. Because they were in space all summer, the astronauts missed out on swimming and picnics back on Earth.

When did this story take place? _____

Where did this story take place? _____

Make a Map!

Think about a character in a story or book that you have read. The character or characters may have taken a journey or simply walked around their town. Where did the main events in the story take place? Using a separate sheet of paper, create a detailed map showing the place where the characters in your story lived.

1. Draw the outline of your map on a sheet of paper.

2. Be sure to write the title and the author of the book at the top of the map.

3. Think about what places you want to include on your map and draw them.

4. Label the important places, adding a brief phrase or sentence about what happened there.

5. Add color and details.

6. Share your map with friends, and tell them about the book you read.

Travel Brochure

A travel brochure gives information about interesting places to visit. Travel brochures usually include beautiful color pictures and descriptive sentences that make people want to visit that place. They also give useful facts about a place.

Plan a travel brochure for the **setting** of a book you have read.

First, brainstorm and write down some ideas about the setting in your book. What would you want to talk about in your travel brochure: What it looked like? local plants and animals? an unusual restaurant? interesting places to visit there?

Then take a sheet of paper and fold it into three sections. You can write on both the front and the back.

Color your brochure with crayons or markers.

Then share your brochure with friends, and tell them about the setting of the book you read.

Extra! Extra! Read All About It!

Newspaper reporters have very important jobs. They have to catch a reader's attention and, at the same time, **tell the facts**.

Newspaper reporters write their stories by answering the questions **who**, **what**, **where**, **when**, **why**, and **how**. Think about a book you have just read and answer the questions below.

Who: **Who** is the story about?

_____

What: **What** happened to the main character?

_____

Where: **Where** does the story take place?

_____

When: **When** does the story take place?

_____

Why: **Why** do these story events happen?

_____

How: **How** do these events happen?

_____

Extra! Extra! Read All About It!

Use your answers on the previous page to write a newspaper article about the book you read.

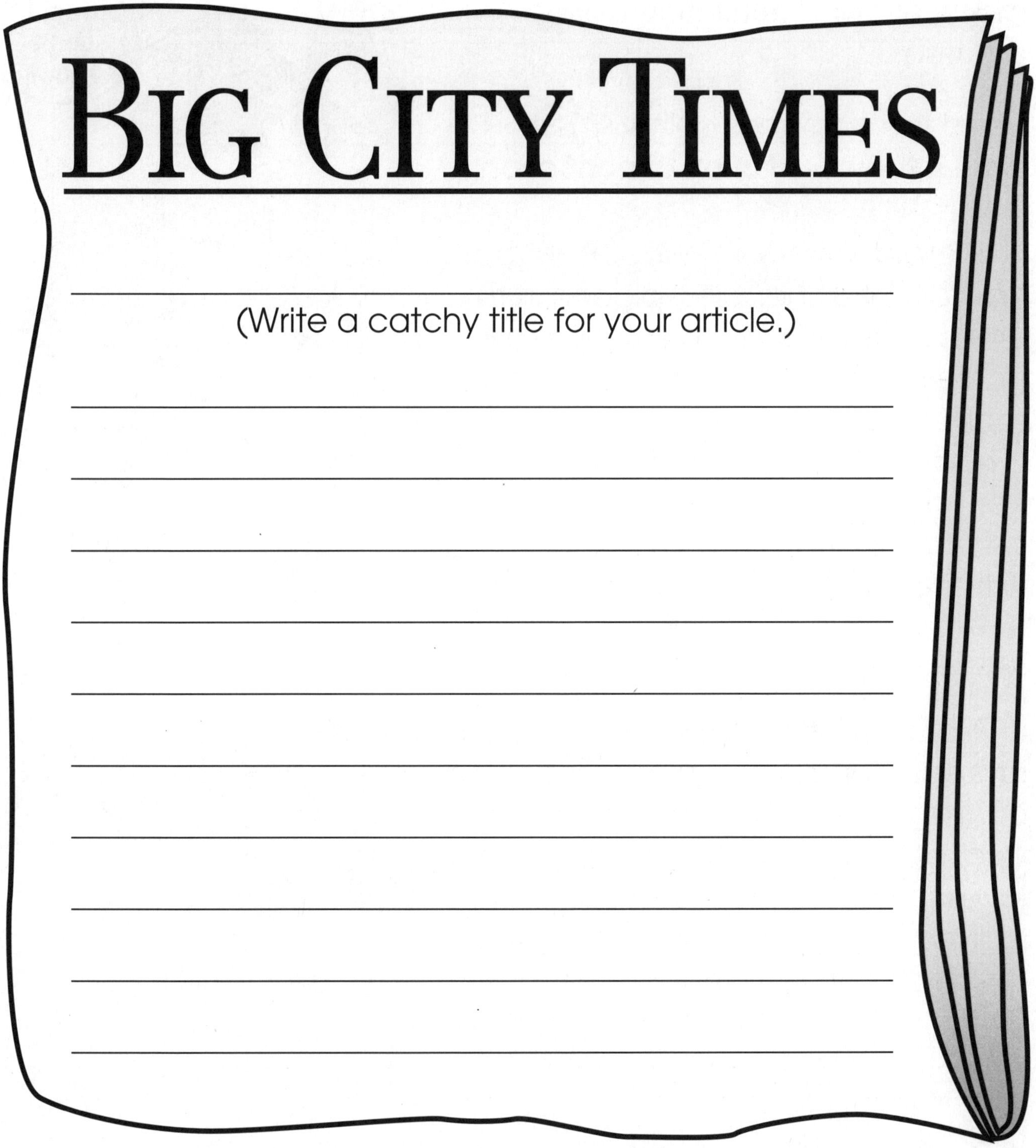

BIG CITY TIMES

_____

(Write a catchy title for your article.)

_____

_____

_____

_____

_____

_____

_____

_____

_____

_____

Fiction or Nonfiction?

Some stories are imaginary, and some are true. **Fiction** stories are made up, and **nonfiction** stories are true.

Is it true?

Gee, I don't know!

Read the passages below. Then write if they are **fiction** or **nonfiction**.

Giorgio was very unhappy. In fact, he was the unhappiest pigeon in the entire world. He was tired of living in traffic lights and in gutters on people's roofs. More than anything he wanted a home, a real pigeon home, with a front door. He was sick of flashing lights and rusty metal gutters, so he came up with a plan.

_____

A platypus is a very strange animal. It swims, lays eggs, and has webbed feet and a wide bill, like a duck! It lives in eastern Australia in lakes, rivers, and streams where it loves to hunt for shrimp to eat. When it dives underwater, it closes its eyes and ears and depends on its touch-sensitive bill to find food.

_____

 Step-by-Step Car Wash

"Hey, Tim! Will you help me wash the car today?" asked my dad.

"Sure, Dad," I answered.

"Great, let's get organized!"

Below are the steps you need to follow to wash a car, but they are all mixed up. Number the steps in order. Mark an **X** in front of any steps that are not needed.

_____ Let the car dry in the sun.

_____ Bring the hose over to the car.

_____ Pick a sunny day (not a rainy day)!

_____ Eat a hamburger.

_____ Move the car out of the garage into the driveway.

_____ Fill the bucket with soap and water.

_____ Brush your hair.

_____ Rinse the car again.

_____ Dance around the car.

_____ Wash down the car with water for the first rinse.

_____ Take a big sponge, dip it into the soapy water, and make slow circles with the sponge to clean the car.

Story Sequence

Read the story. Then write the correct answer to each question.

Aunt Matilda's House!

It was fun spending a rainy Saturday at my Aunt Matilda's house. First, Aunt Matilda said, "Samantha, we can't possibly start our day without a sufficient breakfast! James, chop-chop!" Then her butler, James, brought us two huge crystal goblets of hot chocolate with mountains of whipped cream on top.

After we had finished, Aunt Matilda said to James, "Next, we must have our hair done properly. Send for François, James." Her hair dresser, François, fixed our hair by piling it very high on our heads. "Now," she said, "we must go roller-skating."

"But Aunt Matilda, it is raining outside," I reminded her.

"Don't be silly, Darling. I have a private roller-skating rink downstairs. But first, we need some company. James, let Fifi and Lovey meet us at the rink."

"Yes, Madame," James answered. Then he brought Aunt Matilda's two white poodles to the rink. After that, he put roller skates on all of their feet so they could skate with us!

"Wonderful," said Aunt Matilda, "now we are ready for a proper rainy day!"

That was the best rainy Saturday I've ever had!

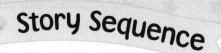

Story Sequence

Put the events listed below in proper order with **1** being the first event and **6** being the last event:

_____ Samantha and Aunt Matilda got their hair done by François.

_____ James brought Fifi and Lovey to the roller-skating rink.

_____ Samantha reminded Aunt Matilda that it was raining outside.

_____ Then everybody was ready for a proper rainy day.

_____ James put roller skates on the dogs' feet.

_____ Aunt Matilda and Samantha drank hot chocolate with mountains of whipped cream.

Detecting the Sequence

Read the story. As you read it, look for clues that let you know the order in which things happened. Then circle the letter choice that best answers each question about the sequence of events.

Beachcombing on Block Island

Beachcombing on Block Island was my favorite family vacation. We took our boat to Block Island, which is a beautiful, tiny island off the coast of America's smallest state, Rhode Island. We docked our boat at Champlin's Marina and got ready to go to the beach.

My dad lifted our bikes off the boat and onto the dock. Then he handed us our backpacks, each filled with a towel, a bottle of water, and a small pail for collecting shells. "Does everybody have a hat?" called my mom. Then she made us put on sunscreen before we rode our bikes to the beach.

Once we got to the beautiful, wide stretch of beach, we unzipped our packs and took out our lucky pails. "Are you ready?" I asked my brother, and he nodded. Then we began our day of beachcombing.

Block Island has beautiful stones and tiny shells that wash up from the Atlantic Ocean. The shells look like small, pink fans. Our pails filled up fast, and we were grateful for a sunny, wonderful Block Island beachcombing day!

Detecting the Sequence

What happened first?

A) The children went beachcombing.

B) The family docked their boat.

C) The family piloted their boat to Block Island.

After the family docked their boat at the Marina, what happened?

A) Everybody put on sunscreen.

B) The father lifted the bikes onto the dock.

C) The father handed the children their backpacks.

When did the children unzip their backpacks?

A) After they got to the beach.

B) When they got on their bikes.

C) When they left the boat.

What happened last at the beach?

A) Their pails were filled with shells.

B) They went back to the boat.

C) They put on more sunscreen.

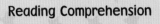

Mimi Gets the Main Idea!

I've got it!

The **main idea** is what a story is about. Help Mimi figure out the main idea of the passages below. Write a check mark next to each main idea.

I write in my diary every night. It helps me remember things, like the places I have visited and people's names. I also write down my feelings in my diary, which helps me feel better.

_____ Everyone has a diary.   _____ Diaries are secret.

_____ Writing in a diary can be helpful.

Leslie is a great athlete, a talented singer, and a good student. Leslie is also a good friend of mine.

_____ Leslie is nice.   _____ Leslie is good at many things.

_____ Leslie is 7 years old.

Mr. Parson eats chocolate all the time. He has hot chocolate for breakfast, chocolate cookies for lunch, and a chocolate bar for a snack. He even has chocolate milk with his dinner!

_____ Mr. Parson has cavities. _____ Mr. Parson loves chocolate.

_____ Mr. Parson bakes a lot.

Getting the Main Idea

Read the story below. Then circle the letter choice for the sentence that tells the main idea of the story.

Ocelots are small cats that live in grassy plains and forests in South and Central America. However, ocelots are not like your typical house cat. They are slightly larger than house cats. Instead of curling up on your bed like a pet cat, ocelots sleep most of the day high up in trees. Then they hunt at night on the ground.

Ocelots don't eat regular cat food from a tin can either. They like to hunt for tiny mammals, birds, even lizards! Another way ocelots are different from a pet cat is that they like to swim! Most domestic cats don't even like to take a bath! Although ocelots are small cats, they are very different from your typical house cat!

The story tells mainly:

A) The history of ocelots in Central America.

B) What ocelots like to eat.

C) How ocelots are different from domestic cats.

Getting the Main Idea

Read the story below. Then answer the questions on the following page.

In 1940, two boys in Lascaux, France, discovered some cave paintings in a 330-foot cave. Scientists believe the paintings they found are over 15,000 years old!

The pictures found were mainly of animals—deer, wild oxen, horses, and reindeer. It is believed that these animals were painted on the cave walls to bring magic, luck, and success to the hunters before they went on a dangerous hunt for food.

Archaeologists believe that, in ancient times, painting served a very different purpose than it does today. Paintings were not created for decoration. Instead, people living in ancient times painted what they hoped would happen. For example, painting a captured deer with an arrow in it would ensure a hunter's success and survival on a hunt.

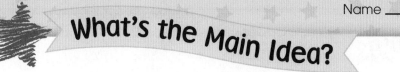

What's the Main Idea?

1. Use one word to name the topic of this passage:

   _____

2. The main idea of the passage is:

   A) Cave paintings were beautiful.

   B) Cave painting began in Lascaux, France.

   C) Cave paintings were most likely painted to bring success to hunters.

   D) Cave paintings were mostly of animals.

3. What were some of the animals found in the cave paintings at Lascaux? _____

   _____

   _____

4. What did it probably mean to an ancient hunter to draw a picture of an animal on the ground with an arrow through it?

   _____

   _____

   _____

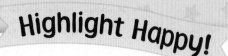

Highlight Happy!

Highlighting is a strategy that will help you with your reading. When you highlight something, you use a light-colored marker to color over a special word or words that you want to remember.

Follow the directions to highlight words in the sentences below.

1. Highlight three states that the Pacific Ocean borders:

   The Atlantic Ocean borders many states on the East Coast of America, such as Connecticut, Georgia, and Florida. However, the Pacific Ocean borders only three contiguous states. Those three states are California, Oregon, and Washington.

2. Highlight two things you should remember:

   You should highlight words or phrases that will help you remember your thoughts.

Goose Bumps!

Name _____

Read the story below. Then answer the questions on the following page.

"Goose bumps! What a funny thing to call those tiny bumps that appear on my arms when I am cold! They make the hair on my arms stand straight up!" I said to my grandpa. "Shouldn't we get human bumps, not goose bumps, if we are cold?!"

My grandpa laughed and said, "Well, Zoe, do you know why we get goose bumps?"

"No," I answered.

"Our skin has hair on it, and when we get cold, the hairs stand up to try to trap more air and keep us warm. Our ancient relatives probably had more hair than we do, and this was a smart way to stay warm," said Grandpa.

"What's so great about trapping air?" I asked.

"If air can be trapped, it is a good insulator, like a padded winter jacket. Other mammals and birds get goose bumps, too, which fluffs out their feathers or fur. This helps the animals trap air and stay warmer," answered Grandpa.

"That's great, Grampa, but I still don't want to be a goose!" I said.

"Okay, well, how about just being a silly goose?" he teased.

"Grampa!" I protested, as we laughed together.

Goose Bumps!

Answer the questions below.

What are goose bumps? _____

Highlight where you found the answer.

What does Zoe think goose bumps should be called instead?

_____

Highlight where you found the answer.

Why do the hairs on our skin stand up? _____

_____

Highlight where you found the answer.

What is so great about trapping air? _____

_____

Highlight where you found the answer.

When animals get goose bumps, what happens to their fur or feathers? _____

_____

Highlight where you found the answer.

Piano Lessons for Priscilla

Priscilla just started taking piano lessons. Her new teacher is named Mrs. Dodd. Mrs. Dodd is very nice, but she lets Pricilla know that learning to play the piano takes hard work and practice. Mrs. Dodd says if Priscilla is serious about becoming a great piano player, she must practice for half an hour every day. Also, she must learn her scales starting with middle C.

What is the main idea this story? Circle your choice.

A) Learning to play the piano takes hard work and practice.

B) Mrs. Dodd is a nice piano teacher.

C) To be a great piano player, you must learn your scales.

What is one thing Mrs. Dodd says you must do to become a great piano player? _____

_____

Eddie the Computer Wizard!

My friend Eddie is a computer wizard! Everybody at my school knows to call Eddie if they have any problems with their computers. People call him "Eddie the Computer Wizard" because he is so knowledgeable about all kinds of computers and programs. He once built a computer all by himself! He also knows how to debug computers and write difficult programs. Parents, teachers, and even the principal have called Eddie for his computer help! Eddie truly is a computer genius.

What is the main idea of this story? Write your answer.

_____

_____

Choose two supporting details and write them below.

_____

_____

Who has called Eddie for help? _____

_____

Cause and Effect

Cause: An action or act that makes something happen.

Effect: Something that happens because of an action or cause.

Look at the following example of cause and effect.

Cause: We left our hamburgers on the grill too long.

Effect: Our hamburgers were burnt!

Read the story below. Then write the missing effect.

Jim and his dad love to go fishing on Sunday mornings. They like to fish when the lake is quiet and most people are still sleeping. Jim and his dad use special bait to catch fish. They have experimented with almost every type of bait and have finally found the one that fish like the best. When they use night crawler worms, they always catch a lot of big fish!

Cause: Jim and his dad use night crawler worms for bait.

Effect: _____

How Did It Happen?

Name _____

Read the stories below. Then write the missing cause or effect.

Joey ate all the cookies his mom had baked. When Joey opened up his lunch the next day, there was a sandwich, an apple, and no dessert. When Joey came home in the afternoon, he asked his mom why she didn't pack him any dessert. "I think you know the answer to that question already!" replied Joey's mom, shaking her head.

Cause: Joey ate all the cookies his mom had baked.

Effect: _____

Going camping in the wintertime with the Boy Scouts takes a lot of preparation. Wearing layers of clothing and waterproof boots are an important part of keeping warm. Bringing a sturdy tent and dry wood is also an essential part of being prepared. Because the Boy Scouts are so prepared, they always have a great time!

Cause: _____

What was the **effect**? _____

Name _____

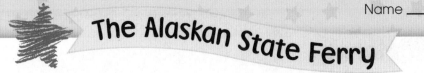

There are many ways to travel to Alaska. Most people visit by taking a plane ride. However, one of the most exciting ways to travel to Alaska is to take the Alaskan State Ferry.

The ferry ride from Seattle, Washington, to Juneau, Alaska, takes three days. It is possible to rent a cabin to sleep in while you're on the ferry, but the cabins get reserved very quickly. Many people who do not reserve a cabin sleep in tents! That's right! Travelers are allowed to set up tents on the deck of the ferry! Even if cabins are available, some people prefer to sleep in a tent because they get to sleep outside under the stars.

It is so much fun to sleep in a tent on the boat, but it is very windy on the deck at night. People are afraid their tents will collapse or blow away, so they tape their tents to the boat with many layers of strong duct tape.

Taking the ferry to Alaska and sleeping under the stars is a ride you will never forget!

Cause: People are afraid their tents will blow away.

Effect: _____

Cause: _____

Effect: People get to be outside and see the stars.

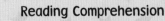

Visiting the Taj Mahal!

Jyoti and Deepa went to visit their grandma and grandpa in the city of Mumbai, India. Their grandparents were very happy to see them. They said, "We have much to show you in India. First, you both must see the Taj Mahal. It is one of the most beautiful buildings in the world."

They took a plane ride and then a car ride to the Taj Mahal. The car ride was very long and hot. Jyoti asked, "Could we open the windows to get some air in the back seat?" Jyoti's Grandma Sindhu nodded. Then Jyoti opened the window, which made the back seat cooler.

When they arrived at the beautiful building, Deepa gasped, "It is very beautiful! I must take a picture!"

"Yes, it is," replied Grandpa Sudhir. "Shaha Jahan built this for his beloved wife, Mumtaz Mahal. She is buried here in this mausoleum. It is disrespectful to walk inside with shoes on." Everybody began taking off their shoes before entering the mausoleum.

"Oweeee," said Jyoti. The marble floor outside the entrance was extremely hot from the sun and burned her feet when she walked on it. Suddenly, Jyoti and Deepa started jumping and hopping on the hot marble.

"What are you girls doing?" asked their grandpa.

"Grandpa, the floor is too hot!" said Jyoti.

"Come on, girls, it's time to get a cool drink and some lunch!" said their grandma, laughing.

Visiting the Taj Mahal!

Refer to the story on the previous page. Use the information to write the missing cause or effect.

Cause	Effect
Jyoti and Deepa visited their grandparents.	_____
_____	Jyoti asked if she could roll down the window.
Jyoti opened the window.	_____
Deepa thought the Taj Mahal was beautiful.	_____
_____	Everybody took off his or her shoes.
_____	The marble floor outside the entrance was very hot.
Jyoti and Deepa burned their bare feet.	_____

Strings Attached!

Draw a line to connect each string of words on the left with a string of words on the right to make a complete sentence. Make sure that each sentence you form makes sense.

The Olympic skier	was an exciting time in history.
The English Knight	can prevent you from sleeping.
Drinking lots of coffee	and loved to make crazy faces.
The comedian was silly	takes a lot of energy, hard work, and perseverance.
The California Gold Rush in 1849	was very well-mannered.
Running for President	was very athletic and loved challenges.

Best Guess!

Read each story below. Using the information from the story, answer each question.

Aisha's teacher was very strict, especially if students were late for her class. She made students stay in for recess for three reasons: if they were late; if they forgot to bring their work; or if they didn't have a pencil. Today, Aisha was early to class and had two sharpened pencils. However, she had left her homework at home on the kitchen table.

What do you think will happen? Circle your answer choice.

A) Aisha's mom will bring her homework to school.

B) Aisha will stay in for recess.

C) Aisha will bring a pack of pens tomorrow.

Nedra loves to eat jellybeans. She eats jellybeans all day long, every day! Her mom told her to stop eating jellybeans or else she will get cavities. Today, Nedra has a dentist appointment...

What do you think will happen at the dentist's office?

_____

_____

_____

Firelight Place

Summer nights at the McMahons' cottage were like nothing my family had ever experienced. The McMahon family had invited our family to spend the weekend at their old summer cottage.

Their cottage was named *Firelight Place*. It was a white wooden cottage with a huge, creaky deck. It sat on the green grass a hundred feet from the lake.

When evening came, all the adults started to grill hamburgers, and chicken, and boiled twenty ears of corn on the cob! All the kids sipped lemonade and iced tea on the deck while watching the stars peek out of the night sky.

"Mrs. McMahon, why is your cottage called *Firelight Place*? It seems too hot to build a fire tonight," I said.

"What a wonderful question," she answered and went inside the cottage. When she came back, she was carrying a tray of empty mayonnaise jars. She gave everybody (adults too!) an empty mayonnaise jar with a plastic lid that had been punctured with many tiny holes. "Attention, everybody!" she said. "Christine wants to know why we call this cottage *Firelight Place*."

Then the entire McMahon family left the deck and walked out into their huge yard. Little red bursts of light flickered on the lawn. Suddenly, the red flickering lights became stronger and brighter.

My family took our jars out to the lawn and joined them. Mrs. McMahon was running around the lawn, laughing. "In the hot

Firelight Place

summer evenings, the fireflies come out and glow red. We catch them in mayonnaise jars to make firefly lanterns. We release them at the end of the night. Yet, for a single evening, they make the most beautiful firelight lanterns!" she said.

Both our families spent the rest of the night laughing, catching fireflies, and making lanterns on that wonderful summer evening.

Answer the questions below.

What time of day was it? _____

What season was it? _____

How long did Christine's family stay at this cottage? _____

_____

How many people do you think are staying at the cottage for the weekend? _____

Choose two words that describe Christine: _____

_____

Choose two words to describe Mrs. McMahon: _____

_____

Why was the McMahons' cottage named *Firelight Place*?

_____

Figure It Out!

An **idiom** is a **figure of speech**. An idiom phrase means something different than what the words actually say. After each sentence, put an **X** in front of the best meaning for the **boldfaced** idiom phrase.

I was really frustrated on Monday. First, my alarm clock broke, and I overslept. Next, my mom drove over a nail. We got a flat tire, and I was late for school. Finally, the **last straw** was when I forgot to bring my lunch to school. What a horrible day!

_____ The **last straw** is when a backpack falls apart.

_____ The **last straw** is when a person is pushed to his or her limit and feels angry or frustrated.

_____ The **last straw** is when someone is so frustrated that he or she needs a soda and a straw to relax.

Matt had decided to change his bad habits and **turn over a new leaf**. From now on, he was going to stop watching T.V. and study more.

_____ Matt will go leaf collecting tomorrow.

_____ Matt will rake leaves instead of watch T.V.

_____ Matt will change what he is doing and start fresh to make things different and better.

What's Next?

Draw a picture of what will happen next in the boxes below:

What Happens Next?

Read each paragraph. Predict what will happen next by placing an **X** in front of the best answer.

Susan played soccer all day on Saturday and scored six goals for her team. Her coach asked her to see him before she went home. "I have something to ask you," he said. What did Susan's coach ask her?

_____ He asked her if she likes soccer.

_____ He asked her if she would like to help him coach the younger soccer players.

_____ He asked her what she ate for breakfast.

My cat and dog don't like each other. My cat chases my dog around the house all day. My big dog, Rex, is afraid of my little cat, Buttercup. What should I do?

_____ Buy a gerbil.

_____ Take Rex to karate classes.

_____ (Write your own answer.) _____

Mathemagic!

Carol loves math. She loves how numbers line up on the page neatly and orderly. She thinks there is nothing more beautiful than the shape of numbers.

Carol loves adding and subtracting numbers and can do it faster than almost anyone (including her parents, her grandparents, and even her teachers!). She is a whiz at hard problems and can add the cost of all the groceries in her head. Then she tells her mom the final price of all the groceries before they get to the checkout counter! Carol thinks math is magic!

Predict what Carol likes to draw in art class. _____

_____

Predict how Carol's mom feels about her daughter being so good at math. _____

Predict what might happen if Carol's grocery total doesn't match the cashier's final number. _____

_____

Predict what Carol might do for a job when she grows up.

_____

Name _____

Read each set of directions. Then circle the letter choice that best answers the question about the directions.

There are three words in the left-hand column. To the right of each word are two more words. Choose the one word that means the opposite of the word at the left. Circle your answer choice.

cease   stop, begin

stupendous   terrible, terrific

haughty   proud, modest

You are to find a word that is:

A) the same in meaning

B) the opposite in meaning

C) very easy

You are to choose from:

A) two words

B) four words

C) five words

The word you choose must be:

A) checked

B) circled

C) written

Following Directions

Axel and Adam were making a haunted house in their neighborhood.

"Mom, we need some scary food to give out at our haunted house," said Adam.

"Oh, that's easy. We'll just make Ax Man snacks for all the children to eat!" said Adam's mom.

"Ax Man snacks? Sounds gruesome!" said Axel.

"Gruesome, but tasty! They are really hot dogs in a bun, but you've never see hot dogs look quite like this! The kids will love them," said Adam's mom.

Help Adam and Axel make some gruesome grub by following the directions below:

What you will need: 4 hot dogs, 8 small sandwich rolls, 1 radish, ketchup, a wooden spoon, and a knife.

Use the handle of the spoon to push a hole lengthwise almost all the way through each roll.

Spoon a little ketchup into each hole. Cut each hot dog in half. Then cut a "bed" for a "fingernail" in the uncut end of each hot dog. Slide a hot dog into each roll, exposing the "fingernail." Cut and trim a thin slice of radish to make a "fingernail" and put it in place.

"These are awesome!" shouted Adam and Axel.

"Yup, truly gruesome!" said Adam's mom, giggling.

Riddles and Codes

Use the code to write the correct letter above each symbol. Some letters have been filled in for you. You will find out the answers to three riddles.

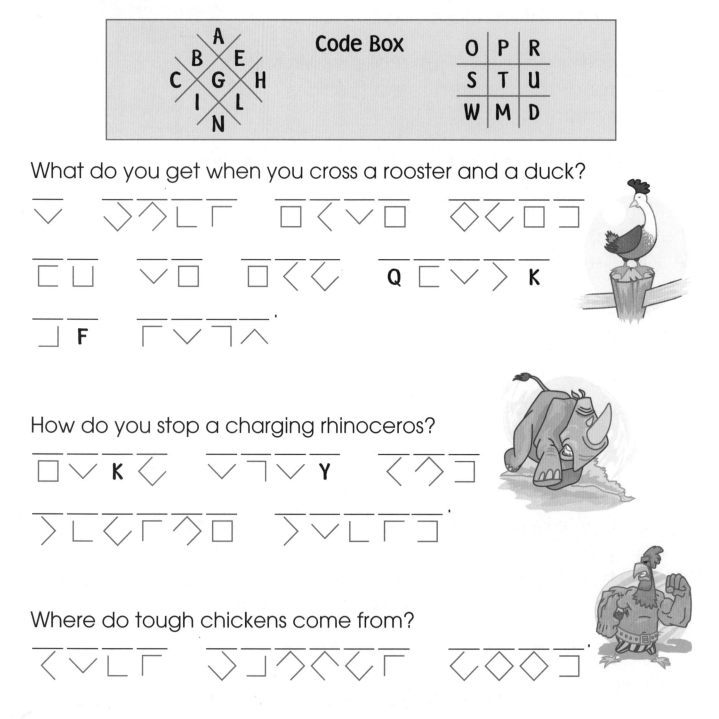

Code Box

What do you get when you cross a rooster and a duck?

How do you stop a charging rhinoceros?

Where do tough chickens come from?

Naming Words—Nouns

A word that names a person, place, or thing is called a **noun**.

person
- magician
- clown
- fisherman

place
- tree house
- bathroom
- closet

thing
- soap
- pail
- leaf

Can you name these nouns?

person _____

place _____

thing _____

Naming Words—Nouns

Complete the story below by filling in the missing nouns. You can use your own words, or you can use the nouns from the word list on the next page. Be sure to read your story aloud after you are finished.

Silly Soap!

"Time to take a bath," called Jeremiah's mom.

Jeremiah hated to take baths. "I wish I didn't have to take baths," he said.

Just as he was about to step into the (1)_____, a (2)_____ popped up from the (3)_____ and said, "Your wish can come true with this bar of (4)_____!"

"Wow, cool!" said Jeremiah while he used it. Soon, his face was totally green!

"Oh, my goodness!" said Jeremiah's mom when he came out of the (5)_____. "You need to take another bath!"

Again, Jeremiah used the bar of (6)_____, and this time he turned green and purple. "This is horrible!" shouted his mom. "No more baths for you!" Jeremiah just smiled.

The End

Naming Words—Nouns

Name _____

Word List

(1) bathtub, birdbath, pool, fountain, sprinkler, washing machine, sink

(2) genie, troll, wizard, leprechaun, clown, magician, squirrel, seal, salmon, fairy, fisherman

(3) drain, floor, basin, secret passage, hole, opening

(4) soap, gold, magic, seaweed, goop, leaves, dirt

(5) bathroom, closet, pool house, spa, tree house, laundry room, backyard, kitchen

Action Words—Verbs

A word that tells what is happening in a sentence is called a **verb**. Verbs are **action words**. Write an action word in each blank. Use the word list to help you.

Word List

discovers	eats	shoots
dances	drives	

Duffy _____ his new, red car.

The lady _____ on the stage.

Coby _____ the arrow at the target.

Judy _____ pumpkin pie.

The archaeologist _____ the hidden doorway.

Word List

creates	builds	scrubs
hammers	mows	

Choose two action words that you like from the word list above. Then write a sentence using each one on the lines below.

_____

_____

Describing Words—Adjectives

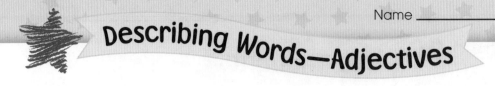

A word that **describes** a noun is called an **adjective**. Adjectives tell what something is like. Fill in each blank below using the adjectives from the word list.

Word List		
tiny	lumpy	pink
spotted	scary	

Although the diamond was _____,
it sparkled like a huge spotlight.

"This bed is really uncomfortable. It is too
_____!" said Max.

The _____ monster in my living room
was only a dream.

The _____ black and white dog is
called a Dalmatian.

"_____ is my favorite color!" said the princess.

Sentences—Complete Thoughts

A **sentence** has a **beginning** and an **ending**. A sentence tells a **complete thought**. When you write a sentence, make sure that all of it is there! Just a beginning or just an ending is not a complete sentence!

"I just don't feel complete."

Draw a line from each sentence's beginning to its correct ending so that each sentence makes sense.

Summer   has thorns on its stem.

My pet turtle   runs fast.

The cheetah   is Kim's favorite color.

A rose   is my favorite season.

Blue   eats a lot!

Sentence Starters

Write an ending for each of these sentences.

A magic squirrel _____

_____

Three balloons flew over my house _____

_____

The rhino's name was Mrs. Ha-Ha, and she _____

_____

Something was strange about _____

_____

I fell asleep on _____

_____

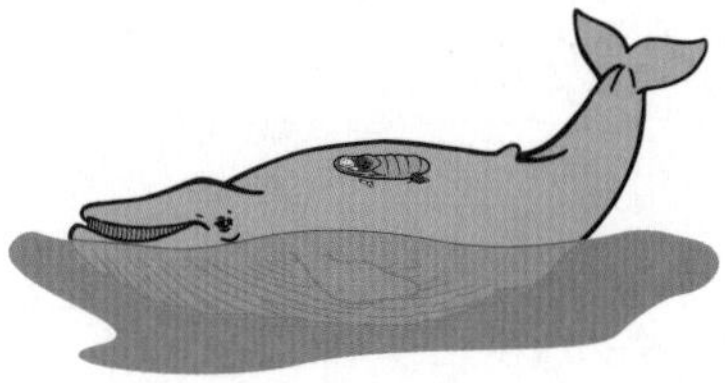

Sentence Endings

Write a beginning for each of these sentences.

_____

_____ was a baby turtle!

_____

_____ on the train!

_____

_____ made of cookies.

_____

_____ you won!

_____

_____ in the attic.

Order Words

Order words tell what comes **first**, **next**, and **last**.

First, we bought the tickets.

Next, we drove to the sports stadium.

Last, we cheered for our team!

Read the story below and circle the order words.

Going on vacation with my family was lots of fun! First, we packed our bags for sunny Hawaii. We took bathing suits, beach toys, and flip-flops. Next, we got on the plane and buckled our seatbelts. We flew over lots of beautiful blue water. Last, we landed at the airport, grabbed our bags, and headed for the beach!

Using Order Words

Draw a picture about your favorite vacation. Maybe you went swimming or traveled to a cold and snowy place. Next, write about your picture. Be sure to use the order words **first**, **next**, and **last** in your writing.

_____

_____

_____

_____

Name _____

Introducing the Five Senses

It is important to understand and to use your five senses so that you can fully enjoy the world and all the exciting things in it. The five senses are:

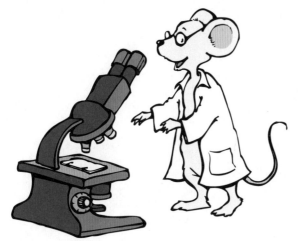

Sight—What you see

Sound—What you hear

Smell—What you smell

Taste—What you taste

Touch—What you feel

The next few exercises allow you to use your fantastic senses. Think about what things might look like, sound like, smell and taste like, and especially, what they might feel like. Have fun!

List three things you can see: _____

List three things you can hear: _____

List three things you can smell: _____

List three things you can taste: _____

List three things you can feel: _____

Sense Exercise—Sight

Look very carefully at the picture below. Study it closely. Then answer the questions on the next page.

Sense Exercise—Sight

Write your answers on the lines below. Your answers will be important clues in helping you tell what happens in the next story.

What does the circus banner say? _____

_____

What are the elephants wearing? _____

_____

What is Herman wearing? _____

_____

How many elephants is Herman lifting in the picture? _____

_____

Who is sneaking up behind Herman? _____

_____

What is the clown doing to Herman? _____

_____

Sense Exercise—Sight

Use your answers from the previous page to fill in the blanks for this story. After you fill in the blanks, keep writing. You will decide what happens in the story.

Herman the Hulking Mouse!

Herman, the hulking mouse, was the strongest mouse in the _____! He could easily lift gigantic _____ dressed in _____. He was the star of the circus and always wore his favorite sneakers and a _____ around his neck.

One day, while Herman was lifting _____ elephants for a huge audience, a _____ decided to play a trick on Herman by _____ his shoelaces together! Herman was having so much fun in the spotlight that he did not notice his sneakers were tied together!

This is what happened next:

_____

_____

_____

_____

_____

_____

Sense Exercise—Sound

Look very carefully at the picture below. Study it closely. Then answer the questions on the next page.

Sense Exercise—Sound

What sound is the woodpecker making in the tree?

_____

What do you think the pet parrot is saying?

_____

What do the squirrels sound like when they crack open the nuts?

_____

What does the breeze sound like through the leaves of the tree?

_____

What does the neighbor's lawn mower sound like when you're up in the tree house?

_____

What do you think the dog's bark is secretly trying to tell you?

_____

Sense Exercise—Sound

Use your ideas from the previous page to fill in the blanks for this story.

The Backyard Tree House!

By _____

"Hey, wait for me!" I called after my brother as he raced up the ladder to the tree house. We climbed as fast as we could to the huge tree house.

"Excuse me," I said when I almost bumped into a _____! He was busily cracking open a nut.

"Wow, the wind sounds _____ all the way up here," said Yoni.

"Everything sounds different this high up. Even Mr. Schmidt's lawn mower sounds like a _____," I replied. Suddenly, it seemed like the whole tree was shaking. We looked down and a _____ was pecking at the tree trunk, making a _____ noise!

Our mom called from the kitchen, "Kids, come down for dinner, please." Our pet parrot was on her shoulder saying, "_____." Then our dog, Coconut, started barking loudly.

Yoni said, "I bet Coconut wants _____!"

The End

Sense Exercise—Smell and Taste

Look very carefully at the picture below. Study it closely. Then answer the questions on the next page.

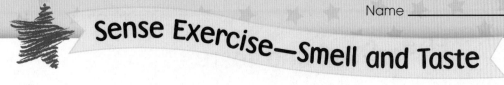

Sense Exercise—Smell and Taste

Write your answers on the lines below. Your answers will help you when you fill in the blanks on the next page.

Do the fish in the nets smell good? _____

What does the air smell like? _____

What do you think the pirates smell like? _____

_____

What toppings do the pirates like best on their pizzas? _____

_____

What is the mouse nibbling on? _____

Does it taste fresh or stale? _____

What is the cat slurping up? _____

Does it taste sweet or sour? _____

Sense Exercise—Smell and Taste

Use your ideas from the previous page to fill in the blanks for this story.

Pirate Ship Pizza!

Black Beard, Red Beard, and Yellow Beard were the three most _____ pirates at sea. They roamed all over the ocean stealing treasures. They forgot to count their food supply, so they ran out of food while they were at sea. Red Beard said, "Don't worry, mates. We will just catch _____ from the ocean until we raid our next ship." The only problem was that all the fish they caught were _____.

"Yuck, these fish smell _____!" said Black Beard, who was so hungry he started to chew on _____. "This tastes _____, even worse than those stinkin' fish!" he cried.

Finally, Yellow Beard said, "I've got a great idea! Let's just order pizza!" Even the cat looked up from her bowl of _____ milk and agreed it was a super idea. The pirates hoisted the international pizza flag high up on the mast. Soon the pizza man delivered three pizzas topped with _____, _____, and _____.

The pirates ate the pizzas and said, "We should order out every day!"

The End

Sense Exercise—Touch

Look very carefully at the picture below. Study it closely like a true adventure seeker. Then answer the questions on the next page.

Sense Exercise—Touch

Write your answers on the lines below. Your answers will help you when you fill in the blanks on the next page.

How would your ears feel when you are deep under the water?

_____

Would the hatch of the submarine be heavy or light to close?

_____

What do you think the starfish feels like? _____

_____

What would a fish feel like against your skin? _____

_____

What would an eel feel like? _____

_____

How would a sea sponge feel in your hands? _____

_____

Sense Exercise—Touch

The House Under the Sea!

My friend lives in an underwater house! One day, he asked if I wanted to come over to his house to play after school. "Sure," I said.

We closed the _____ hatch of his submarine, and we sunk deeper and deeper under the water. Our ears felt _____ going down so deep. Strange-looking fish swam by us. Then we came to his underwater garage. His special garage drained the water around us, so that we could go in his underwater house.

"Do you want to see my pets?" he asked.

We came to a table filled with water and sea animals. "Go ahead and pick one up," he said. First, I picked up a starfish, and it felt really _____ in my hands.

"That's Twinkle," he said. Then a beautiful silver fish brushed by and _____ my hand.

"Oww," I yelled.

"Oh, that's Razor. She is really scaly," he said.

Then I touched this funny-looking plant. "Hey, that _____!" I said laughing. "Your underwater house sure is _____!"

The End

Introduction to Setting—Place

Every story has a setting. The **setting** is the **place** where the story happens. Think of a place that you know well. It could be your room, your kitchen, your backyard, your classroom, or an imaginary place.

Brainstorm some words and ideas about that place. Think about what you see, hear, smell, taste, or feel in that place.

Brainstorm your ideas for a setting below:

Place: _____

_____

_____

_____

_____

_____

_____

_____

_____

_____

Setting—Place

Look at your ideas from the previous page about a setting that interests you and write a paragraph about it. Then draw a picture about your setting in the box below. Remember to include the five senses in your writing.

_____

_____

_____

_____

_____

_____

Name _____

The setting tells the place where the story happens. But the **setting** also tells the **time** in which the story happens. Your reader needs to know when the story is happening. Does your story take place at night? On a sunny day? During winter?

Time can be:

time of day   a holiday   a season of the year

a time in history   a time in the future

The setting also tells the reader **when** the story is happening. Read the letter below. Then answer the questions that follow.

Dear Wendy,

   It is the end of August, and it is almost time for school to start. Soon we will leave our summer cottage. I will miss watching the beautiful sunsets most of all. Well, I'd better go eat my dinner and watch tonight's sunset! See you soon.

Love,

Jeff

What season of the year is it? _____

What time of day is it? _____

Setting—Place and Time

Before you write a story about what happened on the tropical island of Sambamamba, list some words that you could use to describe the setting.

Place	Time
_____	_____
_____	_____
_____	_____
_____	_____
_____	_____
_____	_____

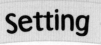

Name _____

Look at your list of words from the previous page describing the island setting of Sambamamba. Now write a setting for your story below that gives your reader a sense of the time and place where the story happens.

_____

_____

_____

_____

_____

_____

_____

Endings

The next few stories have beginnings and middles, but no endings! They need YOU to complete the stories by writing an ending for each one. Use your imagination and what you read in the story to write an ending on page 96. Don't forget to read the stories aloud after you're finished.

Magda's Magic Carpet!

The first thing people noticed when they visited my Aunt Magda's house was her beautiful carpet. It was woven of strange, rich reds and deep purples. "What a beautiful carpet! Where did you get it?" visitors would always ask.

"I got it from an old man in India. He said it was a magic carpet and if I could find the magic word—it would fly! I have said almost every word in the dictionary, and the carpet has never even wiggled!" said my Aunt Magda sadly.

"Aunt Magda," I said one day, "I think I have discovered the magic word! Can I stand on your carpet and say it?"

"Go right ahead," she replied as I stood on the carpet and said…

Name _____

_____

_____

_____

_____

_____

_____

_____

_____

_____

_____

_____

_____

_____

_____

_____

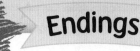

Endings

Name _____

Finish the story below.

The Lost Galleon!

"Long ago, there was a legend of a ship, a mighty captain's galleon, that sunk during a fierce storm at sea. The ship was carrying a queen's treasures—huge emeralds, ruby necklaces, gold statues, and one magical sword," said Calen's scuba guide.

"Local fishermen think the sunken galleon is buried in the murky seaweed bed known as Noman's Reef," said the second guide.

"Why is it called Noman's Reef?" asked Calen.

"Well, because *no man* has ever returned from there," answered the guide.

"Not us. We are going to find that treasure!" said Calen. Then he double-checked his scuba gear and jumped into the rolling sea…

_____

_____

_____

_____

_____

Beginnings and Middles

This story has an ending, but it doesn't have a beginning or middle! Read the ending, and then write a beginning and middle. After you are finished, read your story aloud.

Space Visit!

_____

_____

_____

_____

_____

_____

"Wow! Our planet looks so beautiful from space," I said.

"Yes, it is so blue. I don't think many people get to see Earth like we do!" said Kayla.

"We are so lucky to take this space visit!" I said.

The End

Beginnings and Middles

This story has an ending, but it doesn't have a beginning or middle! Read the ending, and then write a beginning and middle for it.

The Abominable Snowman!

_____

_____

_____

_____

_____

_____

_____

_____

_____

"Do you think we were dreaming, or was it real?" I asked. I felt confused as I stood on the mountaintop.

"No, I think we really saw the Abominable Snowman!" answered Rick as he wiped his forehead with a red bandana. "Look, he even left footprints!" In the wet mud were footprints of a gigantic pair of feet!

The End

Brainstorming

Brainstorming means thinking of everything you can about a topic. Think of a giant storm of ideas coming into your head!

In the "idea clouds" below, write down all the ideas you can think of for the topic, "The Pet Store." Remember, there are no right or wrong words, or good or bad ideas. Just write whatever comes into your brain. Some ideas are already filled in for you.

The Pet Store

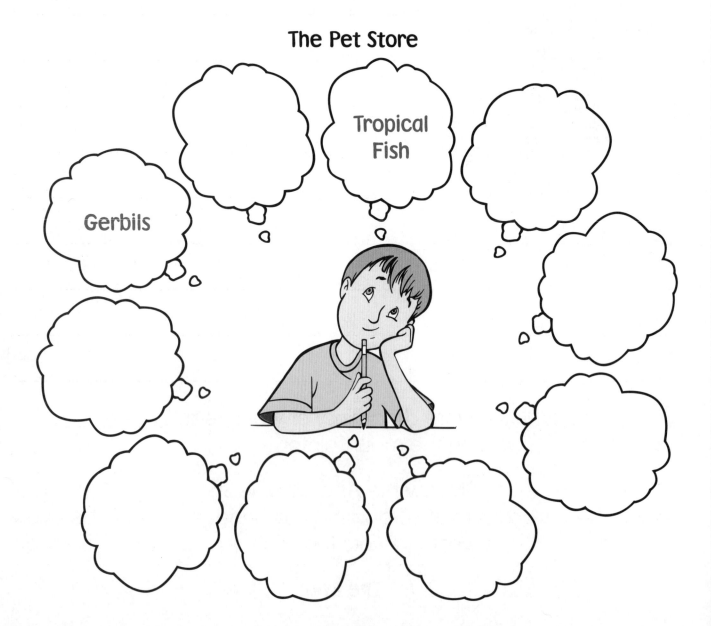

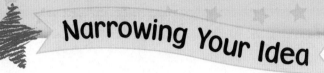

Narrowing Your Idea

Look at your "idea clouds" about the pet store from the previous page. Use a few of your ideas to write a story.

The Pet Store

_____

_____

_____

_____

_____

_____

_____

_____

_____

_____

_____

Name _____

Circle one of the ideas from the list below. Then write down words about that idea.

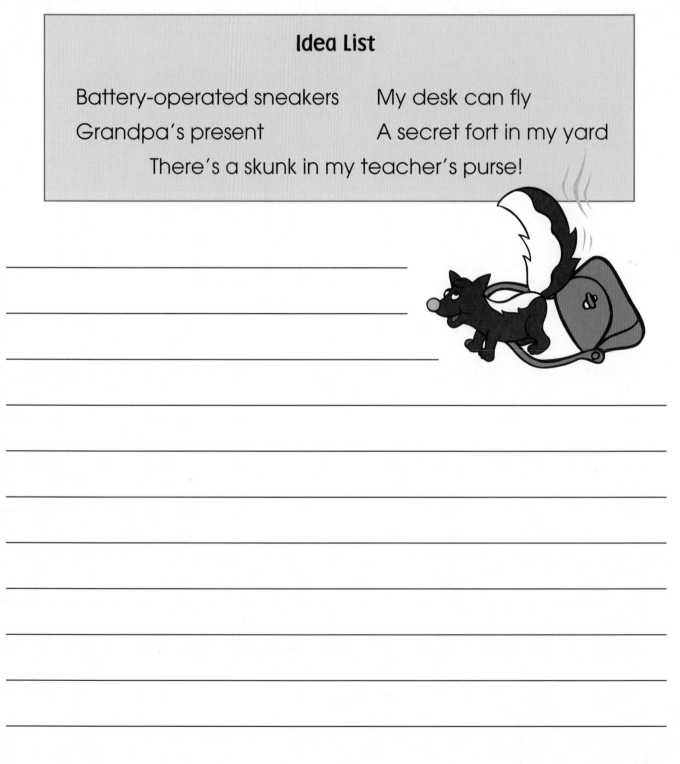

Idea List

Battery-operated sneakers   My desk can fly

Grandpa's present   A secret fort in my yard

There's a skunk in my teacher's purse!

_____

_____

_____

_____

_____

_____

_____

_____

_____

Narrowing Your Idea

Look at your idea list on the previous page. Use your list to help you write a story about the topic you chose.

_____

_____

_____

_____

_____

_____

_____

_____

_____

_____

_____

_____

_____

Story Beginnings

This story has a middle and an ending, but it doesn't have a beginning! Write a beginning for this story.

Genie in a Magic Lamp!

_____

_____

_____

_____

_____

_____

_____

"Those are three wonderful wishes," said the genie, "Good choices!"

"Will they really come true?" I asked.

"You bet! This lamp hasn't been used for 10,000 years! I am just so glad you found me!"

The End

Story Beginnings

The next story has a middle and an ending, but it doesn't have a beginning! Write a beginning for this story.

Swimming With the Dolphins!

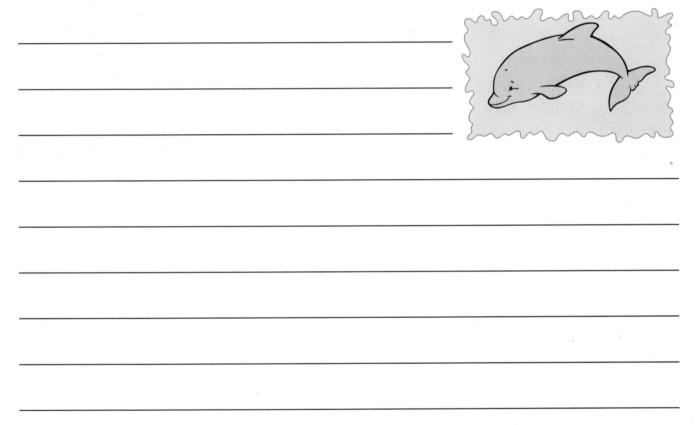

_____

_____

_____

_____

_____

_____

_____

_____

Suddenly, a dolphin appeared next to me and made a happy greeting sound. "Hi there, boy," I said. Then I reached out to stroke his smooth, cool body while I swam. He slowed down and let me grab the fin on his back. Next, we were off gliding through the ocean!

"Samantha, you are so lucky! You get to swim with the dolphins!" my brother shouted from the rowboat. That was the best swim I ever had.

The End

Story Middles

This story has a beginning and an ending, but it is missing its middle! Use your imagination and what you read in the story to write a middle on the lines below. Don't forget to read it aloud after you're finished.

The Magic Lunchbox!

"Only three exist in the whole world," I told my classmates, who gathered around me at lunch.

"Are you sure?" they asked.

"Yes, my father said it was a top-secret project at his lab. First, you put your hand on the lunchbox and ask for any food you want. Then you open it, and the food appears!" I told everybody.

"Let's try! Let's try!" said the group, reaching out their hands to touch the lunchbox.

"Okay, but my dad warned me that the lunchbox hasn't been quite perfected yet...."

_____

_____

"Our principal did not look happy. Oh, my goodness! How will we ever get all of this food out of here?" he said.

"I guess we will just have to eat our way out!" I said.

The End

Story Middles

This story has a beginning and an ending, but it is missing its middle! Write a middle for the story on the lines below.

Balloons to School!

One strange, windy day, a yellow balloon appeared at my front door. I was tired of walking to school, so I said aloud, "Hello, Mr. Balloon. I wish you could fly me to school!"

Suddenly, the balloon moved closer to me and pressed its string against my hand. I held the string in my hand, and the balloon started to…

_____

_____

_____

_____

_____

All the kids ran out of our classroom! "Wow! Look! She's flying!"

The balloon set me down gently outside the classroom. I let go of the string and said, "Thank you, Mr. Balloon." Then the yellow balloon floated away with the next gust of wind.

The End

This story has a beginning and a middle, but no ending! See if you can complete the story by writing an ending below.

Carpet Caper!

Dear Carena

Dear Carena:

I have a very strange problem. My carpet is growing! My bedroom carpet grows higher and higher every day. I can no longer find my shoes or anything else that I leave on the floor! Everything gets buried in the growing carpet. My dad says we should get the lawn mower and mow the carpet. What do you think?

Signed,
Concerned Carpet Kid

Dear CCK,

Many people have this very problem, but they are too embarrassed to tell others about it. Growing carpets are actually quite common. Here is what you should do:

_____

_____

_____

_____

_____

Story Endings

This story has a beginning and a middle, but no ending! Write an ending for the story below.

Gravity-Free Day!

Something was definitely wrong when I woke up on Saturday morning—I was floating! "Hey!" I said, while grabbing my pillow as it floated right by me. I looked around, and my entire bedroom was floating. My desk was floating, my bed was floating, and even my teddy bear was floating!

"Mom! Dad!" I called. "What's happening?" I yelled.

My mom laughed and answered....

_____

_____

_____

_____

_____

_____

_____

_____

Bringing It All Together

What if a holiday were named after you? What would everyone celebrate? Would people celebrate something special you did for the world? Would people celebrate because you had the best smile in the universe? Maybe everyone who has the same name as you do would get the day off!

What would people do on your holiday? Would they eat? Sing songs? March in the streets wearing crazy hats and polka-dotted shoes? Would people go skiing on your holiday? Or stay in bed all day and eat popcorn and gigantic chocolate bars (yum!)? Write (brainstorm!) your ideas on the lines below to get ready to write your own story!

My Holiday!

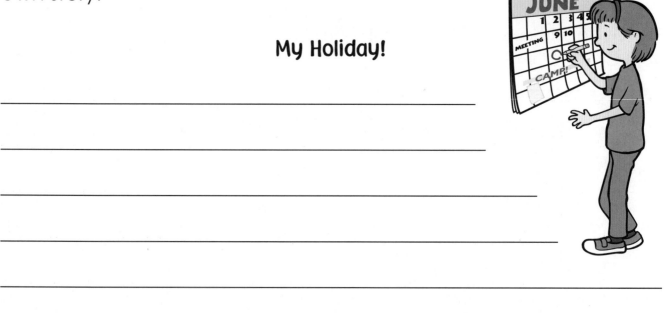

_____

_____

_____

_____

_____

_____

_____

_____

Bringing It All Together

Use your ideas on the previous page to write your own story. Remember, a great story has an exciting beginning, middle, and ending. Good luck!

_____ (title)

By _____

_____

_____

_____

_____

_____

_____

_____

_____

_____

_____

Making It Better—Describing Words

Remember your adjectives! **Adjectives** are **describing words** that give us more information about something. They make our writing more interesting.

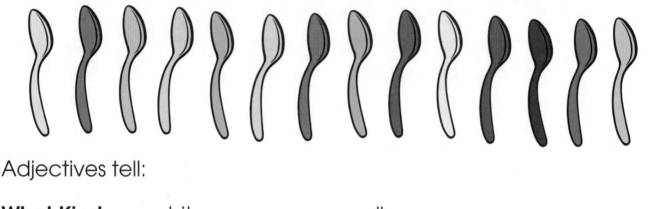

Adjectives tell:

What Kind: white egg   small car   messy room

How Many: five flags   lots of books   a half-dozen donuts

Which One: those ducklings   that lamp   this bowl

Look at each picture and write a word that describes it.

Proofreading—Punctuation

Now that you've added exciting describing words to your story, it is time for a little proofreading! **Proofreading** helps you fix mistakes in **spelling, punctuation,** and **capitalization**.

First, meet Professor Proofhead!

Professor Proofhead would like to show you some exciting proofreading marks.

⬭   misspelling

≡   make a capital letter

⊙   add a period

?   add a question mark

!   add an exclamation mark

It is time to practice proofreading. Use the marks above to proofread the following sentences. The first sentence is done for you.

On m̲onday morning I get up ⟨urlee⟩ ⊙ o̲n ⟨saterday⟩ I sleep late ⊙

I wish I kud fli in a plane two skule i ride the buss

Howe old due yew think I am

Final Draft—With Illustration!

Adjectives help your reader enjoy your story more. Remember, using correct punctuation and spelling makes your story easier to read. Adding describing words, as you did on page 112, helps your reader enjoy your story more.

Go ahead and write the final draft of "My Holiday!" (see page 111), and don't forget to include an illustration! After you are finished, read your story aloud.

_____

_____

_____

_____

_____

_____

_____

_____

_____

_____

Name ______________________________

Final Draft—With Illustration!

Three Things You Like About Your Story!

On the lines below, write three things you like best about your story. Ask yourself: Is my story original? Is it creative? Is it funny? Is it scary? Is my story filled with mistakes, or is it easy to read?

Favorite thing about my story:

_____

_____

_____

_____

Second favorite thing about my story:

_____

_____

_____

_____

Third favorite thing about my story:

_____

_____

_____

_____

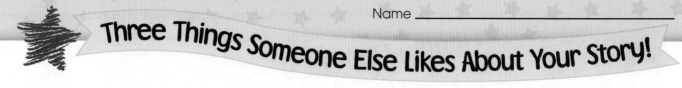

Three Things Someone Else Likes About Your Story!

Have someone read your final draft of "My Holiday!" (see page 114). Then ask him or her to write down three favorite things that he or she liked best about your work.

Most favorite thing about "My Holiday!" by

_____ was:

_____

_____

_____

_____

Second favorite thing about the story was:

_____

_____

_____

_____

Third favorite thing about the story was:

_____

_____

_____

_____

Write a Friendly Letter

Friendly letters are fun to write. It's nice to send letters to friends and relatives. It's also nice to receive letters, too! There are rules for writing certain types of letters. Every type of letter is made up of these parts.

> The letter begins with a **greeting**, usually *Dear*, and the name of the person. Always put a comma after the person's name.

> The **date** must go at the top, right-hand side of the letter.

August 21, 2002

Dear Lynn,

I can't wait to tell you about a story I wrote. It is really exciting, funny, and interesting! It is about a magical lunchbox that gives you any food you wish for—with a few glitches now and then! I hope you like reading my story!

Sincerely,

Spencer

> The letter ends with a **closing**. You can write *Sincerely,* or *Yours truly.* The first word in the closing is always capitalized. Always put a comma after the closing.

> The main part of a letter is called the **body**.

> The writer signs his or her name at the bottom. This is called the **signature**.

Write a Letter Describing Your Story

Look back at one of the stories you wrote. Write a letter to a friend or relative telling him or her about your story. Some parts of the letter are filled in to help you get started.

_____
(date)

Dear_____,
    (greeting)

_____

_____

_____

_____

_____

_____

_____
(body)

Sincerely,
(closing)

_____
(signature)

Just for Fun!

Write a story using all four words listed below. After you are finished, read your story aloud and don't forget to give it a title. Have fun!

Funny Words

pail   shovel

pancake batter   giants

_____ (title)

_____

_____

_____

_____

_____

_____

_____

_____

_____

Just for Fun!

Write a story using one of the ideas below. Then draw a picture to go with your story.

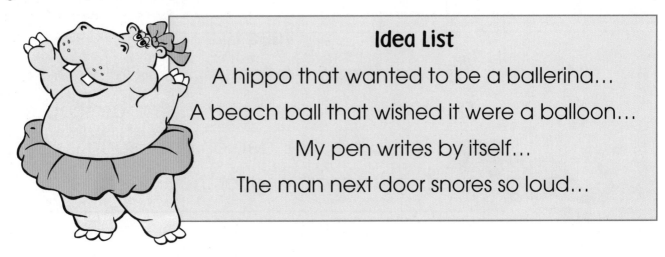

Idea List

A hippo that wanted to be a ballerina…

A beach ball that wished it were a balloon…

My pen writes by itself…

The man next door snores so loud…

_____

_____

_____

_____

_____

Just for Fun!

Write a story using one of the ideas below. Then draw a picture to go with your story.

Idea List

This purple lizard wouldn't stop following me...

Down a secret alley there is a strange shop...

The sailboat landed on the beach...

I went water skiing for the first time....

_____

_____

_____

_____

_____

_____

Picture This!

Take a good look at the pictures below. Choose one of the pictures and write a story about it. Use your own paper for this activity if you need to. Don't just describe the picture. Really think about what is happening, or what happened before or after in the story. Remember this is YOUR story! There is no right or wrong way to write it—only what you want to create. Don't forget to give your story a title and to read it aloud after you're finished.

CHOICE ONE:

CHOICE TWO:

CHOICE THREE:

_____ (title)

By _____

_____

_____

_____

_____

_____

_____

Picture This!

Write a story to go with one of the other pictures on the previous page. Again, remember that this is YOUR story! There is no right or wrong way to write it—only what you want to create. Don't forget to give your story a title and to read it aloud after you're finished.

_____ (title)

By _____

_____

_____

_____

_____

_____

_____

_____

_____

_____

_____

_____

_____

_____

_____

_____

_____

_____

_____

_____

_____

_____

_____

_____

The Carneys' Apartment

The Carneys live in an apartment building. Read the clues to find out the number of their apartment. Each clue will help you eliminate one or more numbers in the chart. Place an **X** on each number you eliminate. The number that is left is the number of the apartment.

Clues: • The number has two digits.

• Both digits are greater than 3.

• The tens digit is greater than the ones digit.

• The sum of the digits is greater than 15.

• The number is even.

What is the number of the Carneys' apartment? _____

1	2	3	4	5	6	7	8	9	10
11	12	13	14	15	16	17	18	19	20
21	22	23	24	25	26	27	28	29	30
31	32	33	34	35	36	37	38	39	40
41	42	43	44	45	46	47	48	49	50
51	52	53	54	55	56	57	58	59	60
61	62	63	64	65	66	67	68	69	70
71	72	73	74	75	76	77	78	79	80
81	82	83	84	85	86	87	88	89	90
91	92	93	94	95	96	97	98	99	100

What a Race!

Use the numbers on the cars to find the mystery number for each clue.

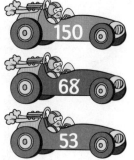

1. I am the smallest two-digit number in the race.

   _____

2. I am the only odd number in the race with 6 tens.

   _____

3. I have the same number of tens and ones.

   _____

4. I have the same number of hundreds and ones.

   _____

5. I have twice as many tens as ones.

   _____

6. I am the only number in the race between 400 and 500.

   _____

7. I am halfway between 100 and 200.

   _____

8. I am the largest two-digit number in the race.

   _____

9. I have two more ones than tens.

   _____

10. I have more tens than either ones or hundreds.

   _____

Number Juggler

Use the digits on the balls to make the four-digit numbers described below. For each number, you must use all four digits.

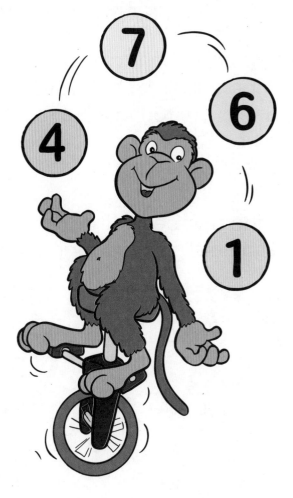

1. Write the smallest four-digit number possible.

_____

2. Write the largest four-digit number possible.

_____

3. Write the smallest number greater than 2,000.

_____

4. Write the largest number less than 2,000.

_____

5. Write the largest four-digit number possible with the 7 in the tens place. _____

6. Write the smallest four-digit number possible with the 1 in the ones place. _____

7. Write the largest four-digit number possible with the 1 in the tens place. _____

Rounding Fun

When you round a number, you tell *about* how many. For example, when 38 is rounded to the nearest ten, it becomes 40. When 32 is rounded to the nearest ten, it becomes 30. Numbers that are halfway between two tens are rounded to the higher number. For example, 35 rounded to the nearest ten is 40.

Use the numbers in the ropes to make two-digit numbers. Don't use the same digit more than once in a number.

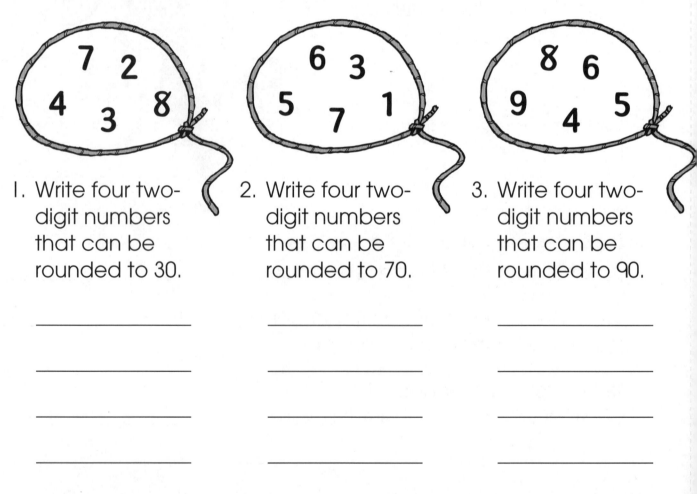

1. Write four two-digit numbers that can be rounded to 30.

_____

_____

_____

_____

2. Write four two-digit numbers that can be rounded to 70.

_____

_____

_____

_____

3. Write four two-digit numbers that can be rounded to 90.

_____

_____

_____

_____

Number Roundup

When you round a number to the nearest hundred, look at its last two digits. If you see 50 or more, round to the higher hundred. If you see less than 50, round to the lower hundred. For example, 256 is rounded to 300 and 245 is rounded to 200.

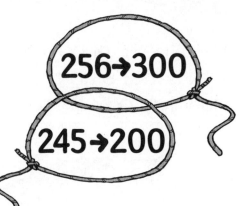

Use the numbers in the ropes to form three-digit numbers. Don't use the same digit more than once in a number.

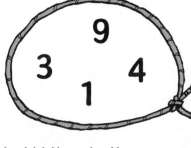

1. Write six three-digit numbers that can be rounded to 400.

_____

_____

_____

_____

_____

_____

2. Write six three-digit numbers that can be rounded to 600.

_____

_____

_____

_____

_____

_____

3. Write six three-digit numbers that can be rounded to 800.

_____

_____

_____

_____

_____

_____

Downhill Climb

Help the hiker get down the hill. Starting at the top, color a path that is made up of numbers that add up to 20. You can travel only downward or diagonally. You may not go backwards up the path.

A Super Duper Bus Tour

Name _____

The Super Duper Bus Company is taking some people on a bus tour. They will be traveling from Anytown to Elk Falls. This map shows where they will be going.

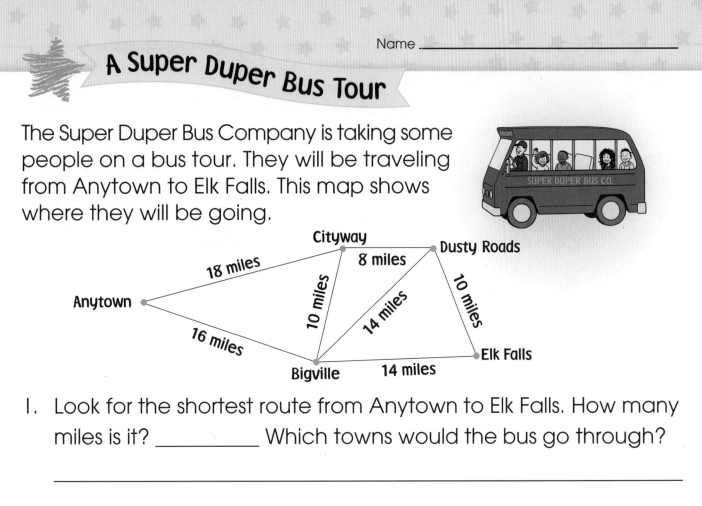

1. Look for the shortest route from Anytown to Elk Falls. How many miles is it? _____ Which towns would the bus go through?

   _____

2. Suppose the bus driver plans to make stops at Bigville, Cityway, and Dusty Roads before arriving at Elk Falls. How long is the shortest route? (No backtracking is allowed.) _____ How long is the longest route? _____

3. Starting with Anytown, list the towns in order that make up the shortest route.

   _____

   _____

4. Starting with Anytown, list the towns in order that make up the longest route.

   _____

   _____

Zoo News

Read the news about the zoo. Then solve the problems.

1. On Monday, 5 classes of children visited the aquarium. Every day after that, the number of classes per day increased by 3. How many classes visited the aquarium on Friday? Fill in the chart to help you get the answer.

	Mon.	Tues.	Wed.	Thurs.	Fri.
Number of Classes					

On Friday, _____ classes visited the aquarium.

2. There were several starfish and octopuses in an aquarium tank. Each starfish had 5 arms. Each octopus had 8 arms. Altogether there were 70 arms in the tank. How many starfish and octopuses were in the tank?

starfish _____

octopuses _____

3. Sammy is a harbor seal and Salty is a sea lion. Both are fed fish every day at the aquarium. Sammy eats 15 pounds of fish a day. Salty eats 25 pounds of fish a day. Fill in the chart to show how many pounds of fish the two animals eat by adding each day's amount.

	Day 1	Day 2	Day 3	Day 4	Day 5	Day 6	Day 7
Sammy							
Salty							

Look at the chart you completed.

After how many days will Salty have eaten 50 more pounds of fish than Sammy did?

_____

After how many days do you think Salty will have eaten 100 more pounds of fish than Sammy did?

_____

Continue the chart from above to prove your answer.

Name _____

Write **+** or **–** in the circles to make the following number sentences true. (Start at the left of each sentence. Then add or subtract in order.)

1. 5 ◯ 2 ◯ 3 = 4

2. 6 ◯ 5 ◯ 4 = 7

3. 12 ◯ 4 ◯ 1 = 7

4. 10 ◯ 9 ◯ 8 = 9

5. 6 ◯ 5 ◯ 4 ◯ 1 = 14

6. 12 ◯ 2 ◯ 10 ◯ 8 = 8

7. 15 ◯ 6 ◯ 4 ◯ 2 = 15

8. 8 ◯ 3 ◯ 6 ◯ 10 = 21

All in the Family

Read the clues. Then figure out the ages of these family members. (Begin by guessing an age; then check it against the clues presented in each problem.)

1. Kim's mom is three times older than Kim. Kim's grandmother is twice as old as Kim's mom. The sum of their ages is 100. How old are Kim, her mom, and her grandmother?

   Kim _____

   Kim's mom _____

   Kim's grandmother _____

2. Mr. and Mrs. Lee have four sons. The boys are all one year apart. The sum of their ages is 30. How old are the boys?

   _____

3. Jenny and Ann are sisters. Jenny is three times older than Ann. In four years, Jenny will be twice as old. How old are Jenny and Ann?

   Jenny _____

   Ann _____

Grocery Store Math

Read the problems and solve them.

1. The grocery store clerk is stocking 100 cans of soup on four shelves. He stocks the cans so that each shelf has two more cans than the one above it. How many cans are on each shelf? Write the answers from top to bottom on the shelves at the right.

Top Shelf _____ cans	
Second Shelf _____ cans	
Third Shelf _____ cans	
Bottom Shelf _____ cans	

2. There are three kinds of bottled juice on display. There are six more bottles of apple juice than there are bottles of cranberry juice. There are four more bottles of grape juice than there are bottles of apple juice. Altogether there are 52 bottles. How many bottles of each kind are there?

grape juice _____

apple juice _____

cranberry juice _____

3. Mrs. Kerr is going to buy some frozen beans. Each bag of beans contains five servings. There are six people in Mrs. Kerr's family. If she wants to serve beans twice this week, how many bags will she need to buy?

_____

4. There are five boxes of pasta displayed in a line. Each box is 10 inches wide. There is a space of 2 inches between each box. How long is the line of boxes? (You may use the picture of boxes below to help you solve the problem.)

_____

5. Mr. Gorman is buying bread and crackers. Each loaf of bread costs $1.30. Each box of crackers costs $1.50. Mr. Gorman goes to the checkout stand and pays $7.10. How many loaves of bread and boxes of crackers does he buy?

_____

6. At 5 o'clock, several customers line up at the checkout stand. Three customers pay and leave as two more customers line up. Then one more customer leaves and four more customers line up. Now there are eight customers at the checkout stand. How many customers were there at 5 o'clock?

_____

Name _____

Help the children find their cat. She is hiding behind one of the rocks. To find the correct rock, start at the top of the path with the number 2. Then follow the lines, multiplying as you go. When all the numbers in the correct path are multiplied, they equal 120. Color the numbers you followed.

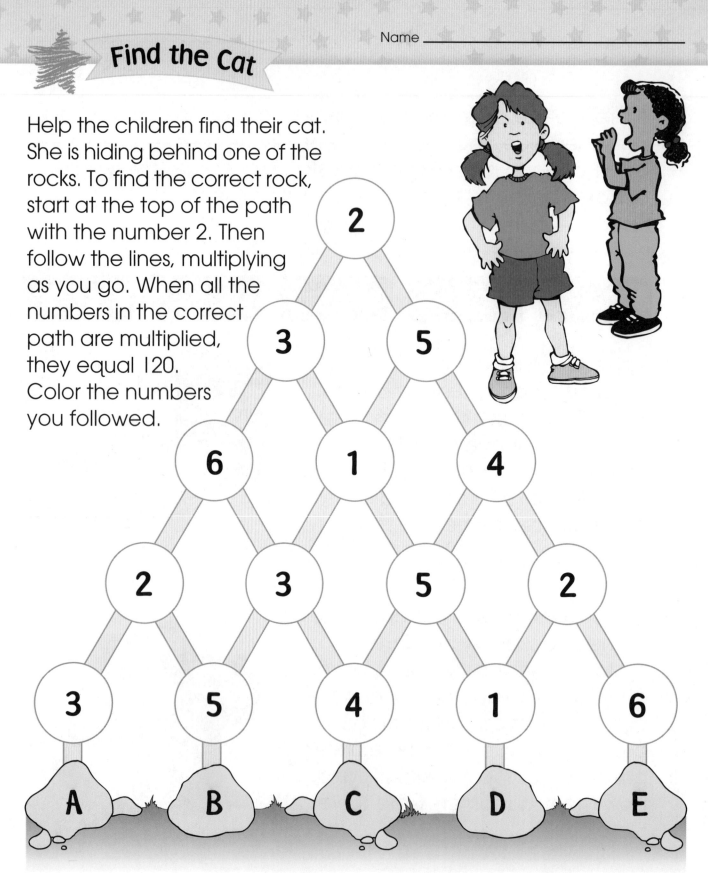

The cat is hiding behind rock _____ .

Fill in the Signs

Write **x** or ÷ in the circles to make the following number sentences true. (Start at the left of each sentence. Then multiply or divide in order.)

1. 4 ◯ 2 ◯ 1 = 8

2. 10 ◯ 5 ◯ 3 = 6

3. 12 ◯ 3 ◯ 4 = 16

4. 7 ◯ 4 ◯ 2 = 14

5. 3 ◯ 4 ◯ 2 ◯ 6 = 4

6. 3 ◯ 4 ◯ 2 ◯ 6 = 1

7. 8 ◯ 2 ◯ 3 ◯ 4 = 3

8. 15 ◯ 3 ◯ 2 ◯ 3 = 30

Toy Car Collections

Barry, Harry, and Larry collect toy cars. Right now, each boy has fewer than 20 cars. To find out how many each child has, read these clues.

1. Barry's Cars

    Divide the number by 2, and you get 1 remainder.
    Divide the number by 3, and you get 1 remainder.
    Divide the number by 4, and you get 1 remainder.
    Divide the number by 6, and you get 1 remainder.

    How many cars does Barry have? _____

2. Harry's Cars

    Divide the number by 2, and you get 1 remainder.
    Divide the number by 3, and you get 2 remainders.
    Divide the number by 4, and you get 1 remainder.
    Divide the number by 5, and you get 2 remainders.

    How many cars does Harry have? _____

3. Larry's Cars

    Divide the number by 2, and you get 1 remainder.
    Divide the number by 3, and you get 1 remainder.
    Divide the number by 4, and you get 3 remainders.
    Divide the number by 5, and you get 4 remainders.

    How many cars does Larry have? _____

Making Numbers

Look at the numbers. Each row is created with numbers that form a certain pattern.

21 → 3

45 → 9

116 → 8

57 → 12 → 3

99 → 18 → 9

Find the pattern above, then use it to complete the rows of numbers below.

26 _____

123 _____

58 _____

809 _____

1,387 _____

Use the same pattern to create your own row of numbers.

_____

_____

_____

Mystery Triangles

1. Look at the number triangle. Figure out the pattern of the numbers. Then fill in the missing number.

30

40   _____

60   20   10

100   40   20   10

2. Here is another number triangle made by the same pattern. Fill in the missing numbers.

24

29   _____

49   _____   15

99   50   30   15

3. Use the same pattern to create your own number triangle.

_____

_____   _____

_____   _____   _____

_____   _____   _____   _____

Triangle Sums

1. Write the numbers 1 to 6 in the circles so that the three numbers on each side of the triangle add up to the same sum.

   1 2 3 4 5 6

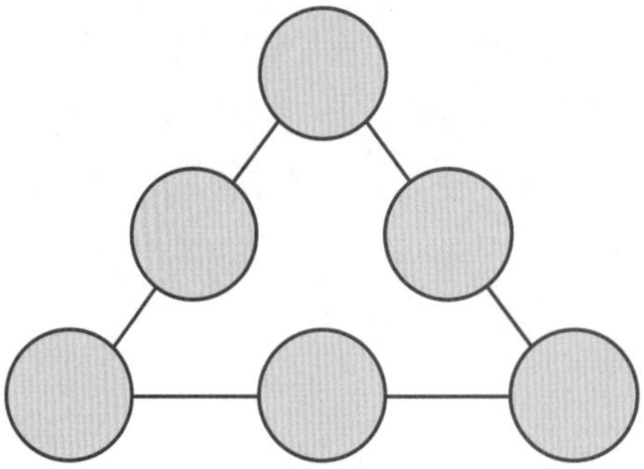

2. Write the numbers 3 to 8 in the circles so that the three numbers on each side of the triangle add up to the same sum.

   3 4 5 6 7 8

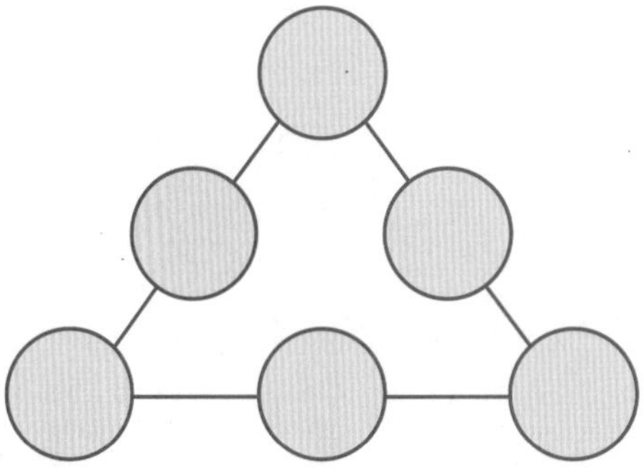

3. Write the numbers 5 to 10 in the circles so that the three numbers on each side of the triangle add up to the same sum.

   5 6 7 8 9 10

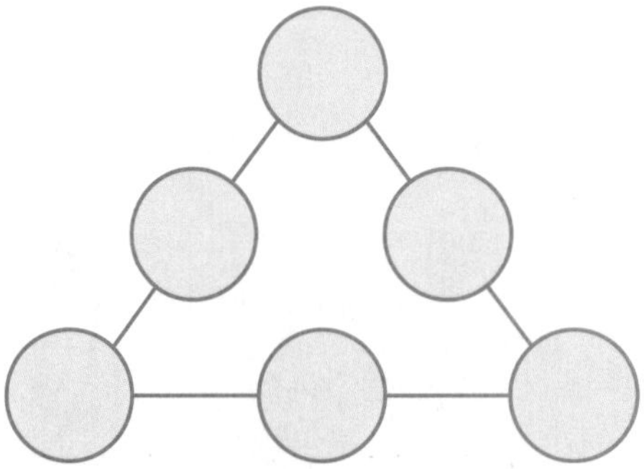

4. Study the triangles. What do you notice about the arrangement of the numbers?

   _____

   _____

   _____

Shell Numbers

These children live in a place where shells are used in place of numbers. Each shell is worth a different value. The values range from 1 to 9. See if you can figure out the value of the shells on this page. Write the matching numbers on the lines.

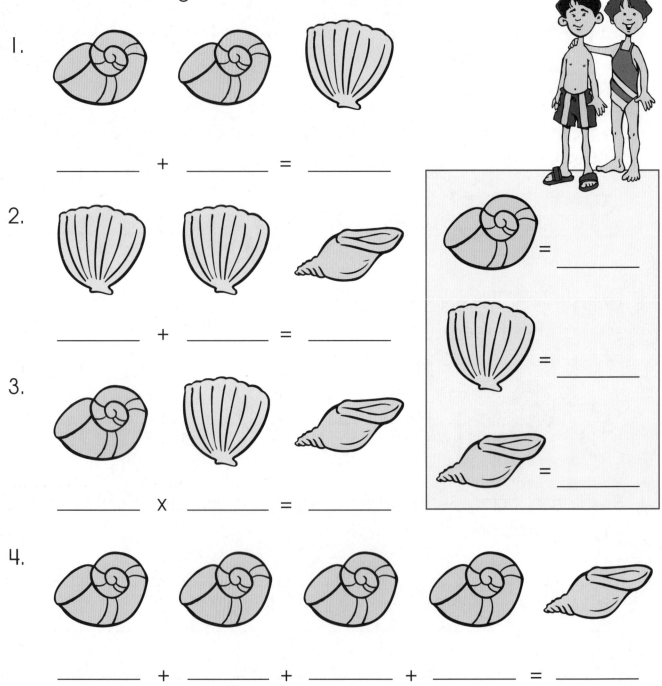

1. _____ + _____ = _____

2. _____ + _____ = _____

3. _____ X _____ = _____

⬡ = _____

🐚 = _____

🐚 = _____

4. _____ + _____ + _____ + _____ = _____

Button Game

Max and Bob are playing a game with buttons. Each button is worth a different value. The values range from 1 to 9. Figure out the value of each button below. Then write the matching numbers on the lines.

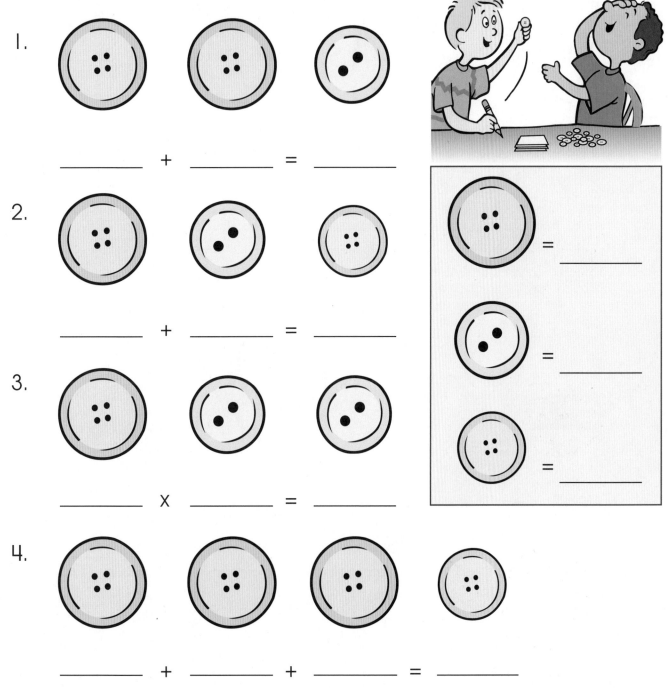

1. _____ + _____ = _____

2. _____ + _____ = _____

3. _____ x _____ = _____

4. _____ + _____ + _____ = _____

What's Next?

Study the figures in each row. Draw the figure that should come next.

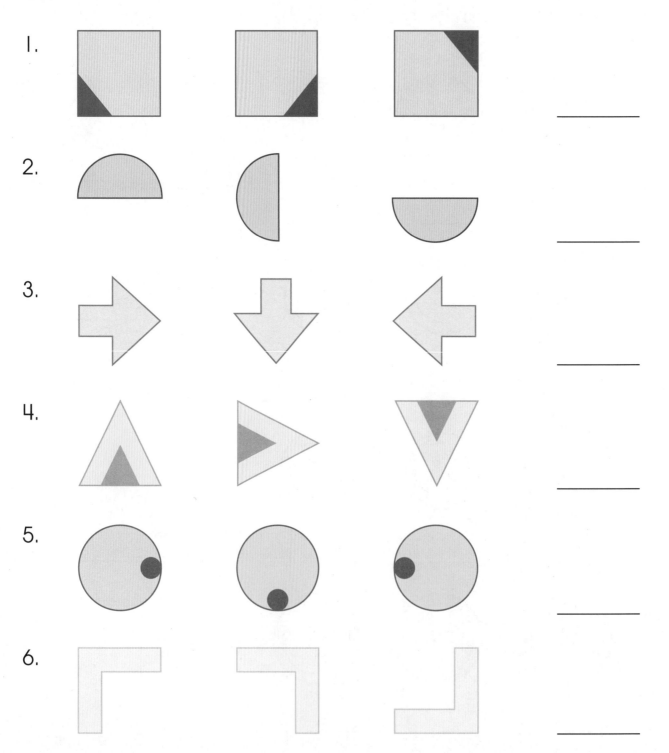

1. _____

2. _____

3. _____

4. _____

5. _____

6. _____

What's in the Piggy Bank?

Read the clues. Draw what is in each piggy bank. Use dollar bills, half dollars, quarters, dimes, nickels, and pennies.

1.  There are four coins. They add up to 80¢.

_____

2.  There are five coins. They add up to $1.00.

_____

3.  There are two bills and three coins. They add up to $3.10.

_____

4.  There are two bills and five coins. They add up to $3.05.

_____

5.  There are three bills and three coins. They add up to $4.25.

_____

Rows of Coins

Read each problem. Write the values of the coins in the circles. Then write the total amount of money on each line.

1. Jessica has six coins. She has only nickels and dimes. Jessica has twice as many nickels as dimes. How much money does she have?

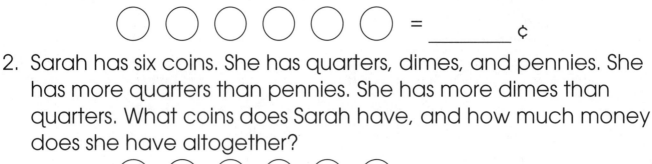

$\bigcirc \bigcirc \bigcirc \bigcirc \bigcirc \bigcirc$ = _____ ¢

2. Sarah has six coins. She has quarters, dimes, and pennies. She has more quarters than pennies. She has more dimes than quarters. What coins does Sarah have, and how much money does she have altogether?

$\bigcirc \bigcirc \bigcirc \bigcirc \bigcirc \bigcirc$ = _____ ¢

3. Scott has four coins that total 70¢. His coin of highest value is a half dollar. Vicky has four coins that total 70¢. Her coin of highest value is a quarter. What coins do they have?

Scott $\bigcirc \bigcirc \bigcirc \bigcirc$ = _____ ¢

Vicky $\bigcirc \bigcirc \bigcirc \bigcirc$ = _____ ¢

4. Amy has two coins. Wendy has three coins. Both girls have the same amount of money. Neither of Amy's coins match Wendy's coins. What are the coin combinations, and how much money does each girl have?

Amy $\bigcirc \bigcirc$ = _____ ¢

Wendy $\bigcirc \bigcirc \bigcirc$ = _____ ¢

Saving Money

Jan and Fran each want to save at least $10.00. Jan will save $1.25 each week. Fran will save 50 cents the first week. Each week after that, she will save 50 cents more than she did the previous week. Who will reach her goal first—Jan or Fran? Fill in the chart to show your answer.

Jan

Week	Amount Saved for the Week	Total Amount Saved
1		
2		
3		
4		
5		
6		
7		
8		

Fran

Week	Amount Saved for the Week	Total Amount Saved
1		
2		
3		
4		
5		
6		
7		
8		

_____ will save $10.00 first.

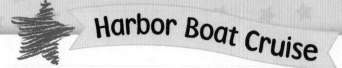

Harbor Boat Cruise

The Harbor Boat Cruise is a popular ride. The boat runs once an hour, and it holds 20 passengers at a time. The ride costs $4.00 for adults and $3.00 for children.

1. For the 2:00 cruise, there were an equal number of adults and children. How much did the boat's captain collect?

   _____

2. For the 3:00 cruise, the captain collected $68.00. There were four more children than there were adults. How many adults and children went on the boat?

   _____

3. Suppose every cruise carried the maximum number of passengers with both adults and children.

   What is the most amount of money the captain could collect?

   _____

   What is the least amount of money
   the captain could collect?

   _____

Cookie Sales

Mrs. White owns a bakery. One morning she puts out several trays filled with cookies.

Mrs. Rogers is the first customer. She looks at the cookies and decides to buy half of them.

Next comes Mr. Grant. He looks at the cookies that are left, and then buys half of them.

Miss Lang enters the shop. She quickly buys half of the cookies she sees.

Finally, Mrs. Soo arrives at the bakery. She buys six cookies. She would like to buy more, but there are no more cookies left.

1. How many cookies did each of the other customers buy?

   Mrs. Rogers _____

   Mr. Grant _____

   Miss Lang _____

2. How many cookies were for sale when the bakery first opened?

   _____

A Marching Band

Here comes the parade! Solve these problems about the marching band.

1. There are 24 members in the band. One-half of them are wearing blue. One-fourth of them are wearing yellow. The rest are wearing red. Color the circles to show how many are wearing blue, how many are wearing yellow, and how many are wearing red.

2. What fraction describes how many members are wearing either blue or yellow?

_____

3. What fraction describes how many members are wearing either yellow or red?

_____

4. What fraction describes how many members are wearing either red or blue?

_____

Rock Hunting

Name _____

Jeff has a rock collection. Every week he goes out hunting for rocks. Each time, 1/2 of the rocks Jeff finds are solid-colored, 1/4 are speckled, and 1/4 are striped. Not only that, but Jeff always finds more rocks than he did the previous week. Fill in the chart below to show how many rocks Jeff finds.

	Solid-Colored	Speckled	Striped	Total Number of Rocks
Week 1	4	2	2	8
Week 2		4		
Week 3	12			
Week 4			8	

1. Look at the total number of rocks Jeff finds each week. What pattern do you see?

_____

2. Look at the number of solid-colored rocks Jeff finds each week. What pattern do you see?

_____

3. Look at the number of speckled rocks and striped rocks Jeff finds each week. What pattern do you see?

_____

4. Suppose the pattern continues. What is the total number of rocks Jeff will find in Week 5?

_____

Toy Animals Display

Look at the toy animals. Then on each line below, write the fraction that makes each sentence true.

1. _____ of the animals have bows.

2. _____ of the rabbits have bows.

3. _____ of the animals are teddy bears.

4. _____ of the cats have stripes.

5. _____ of the animals are either cats, dogs, or rabbits.

Write another sentence that uses a fraction to describe the toy animals.

_____

Colorful Blocks

Name _____

Trevor and Margo each stacked five different colors of blocks one on top of the other. Read their clues and color the blocks to match.

Trevor's Clues:
- Blue is next to green.
- Red is next to blue.
- Red is at the top.
- Yellow is between green and brown.

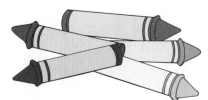

Margo's Clues:
- Orange is between red and blue.
- Red is between orange and yellow.
- Purple is next to yellow.
- Blue is not at the bottom.

A Dog Show

Mandy, Randy, and Sandy entered their dogs in a dog show. Use the clues to find out what kind of dog each child owns and which prize each one took home. Fill in the chart at the bottom of the page to help you.

Clues:
- Sandy's dog did not win first prize.
- Mandy does not have a beagle.
- The collie won first prize.
- Randy's dog won second prize.
- The child with the poodle took home third prize.

Child	Dog	Prize

Name _____

Ice Cream Favorites

Lori, Lily, and Lana are sisters. One girl is eight years old, one is nine, and one is ten. All three girls love ice cream! Use the clues to find out each girl's age and favorite ice cream flavor. Fill in the chart at the bottom of the page to help you.

Clues:
- The girl who likes chocolate ice cream is the youngest.
- Lily is older than Lana.
- The girl who likes vanilla ice cream is older than the girl who likes strawberry ice cream.
- Lori is not the youngest.
- Lily does not like strawberry ice cream.

Child	Age	Ice Cream

Fruit Baskets

Mary is arranging apples, oranges, pears, and bananas into baskets for gifts. Each basket has 12 pieces of fruit. No two baskets are alike. Read the clues. For each basket, list the different numbers of fruits.

1. There is the same number of apples in the basket as there are oranges. There are twice as many pears as there are bananas.

_____ apples

_____ oranges

_____ pears

_____ bananas

2. There is one more apple than there are bananas. There is one more pear than there are oranges. There are more oranges than apples.

_____ apples

_____ oranges

_____ pears

_____ bananas

3. For every banana, there are three oranges. For every pear, there are three apples. There are more apples than oranges.

_____ apples

_____ oranges

_____ pears

_____ bananas

Frog Hop

Hop-Along Frog is playing a game. He is going to hop on the numbered lily pads to get to his friends. As Hop-Along lands on the lily pads, he will add up their numbers.

Hop-Along will not land on a lily pad more than once. He can hop from one lily pad to another only if they are connected. Color the path that will give Hop-Along the greatest sum.

For an extra challenge, use a different color of crayon to color a path that will give Hop-Along the least sum!

Shape Symbols

Each shape stands for a number. See if you can figure out the numbers!

1. Write the number each shape stands for.

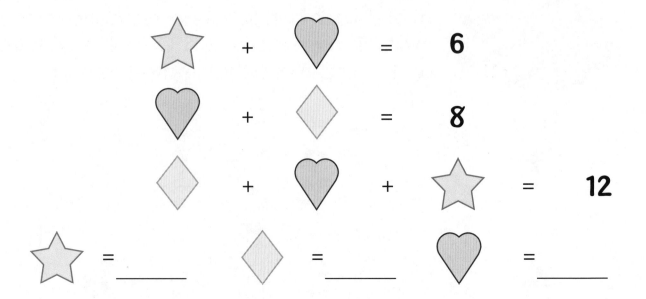

2. Write the number each shape stands for.

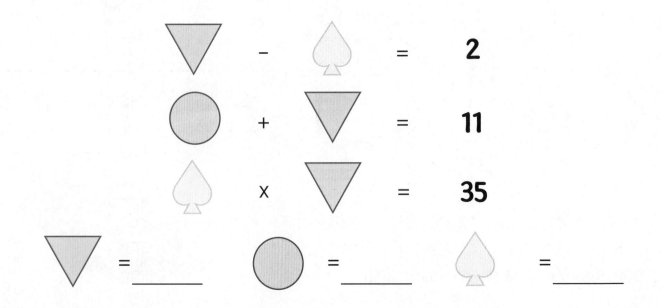

Name _____

Glip's Numbers

Glip lives on a faraway planet. In his homeland, Glip uses shapes when writing numbers. Look at the shapes and the numbers they stand for. Then fill in the numbers for the remaining rows.

1. △ △ △ △ ⌂ ⌂ ⌂ ⌂ ⌂ = **54**

2. ⌂ ⌂ △ △ △ △ △ ⊙ ⊙ ⊙ = **325**

3. ⊙ ⊙ ⊙ ⊙ △ ⌂ ⌂ ⌂ = _____

4. △ △ △ △ △ △ ⊙ ⌂ = _____

5. What does △ stand for? _____

6. What does ⌂ stand for? _____

7. What does ⊙ stand for? _____

Use the shapes to create another number below.

Going on a Field Trip

Tina and Kristy are going to the museum with their class. Solve these problems about their trip.

1. Tina and Kristy are waiting in line to get on the school bus. Tina is seventh in line. Kristy is in the middle of the line. There are six students between Tina and Kristy. How many students are waiting in line?

   _____

2. When the students get on the bus, Kristy heads towards the back. Tina stays near the front. Kristy finds a seat in the third row from the back. Tina finds a seat in the fifth row from the front. There are four rows between the two girls. How many rows of seats are in the bus?

   _____

3. At the museum, the tour guide lines up the class in this pattern: boy, girl, boy, girl, boy, girl. The first person in line is a boy named Jeffrey. Tina is the fifth girl in line. How many students are standing between Tina and Jeffrey?

   _____

Cafeteria Lineup

There are 30 children waiting in line to go into the school cafeteria. Read the following problems and solve them.

1. Every seventh child in the line is wearing a blue T-shirt. How many children are wearing blue T-shirts?

    _____

2. Every fourth child in the line is wearing a white T-shirt. How many children are wearing white T-shirts?

    _____

3. Every fifth child in the line is wearing shorts. Every sixth child is wearing glasses. How many children are wearing shorts and have glasses?

    _____

4. Every third child in the line is going to buy a chicken sandwich. Every fourth child is going to buy apple juice. How many children are going to buy a chicken sandwich and apple juice?

    _____

Cindy's House

Use Cindy's clues to help you find her house. When you find the house, circle it.

Clues: • My house has a chimney.

• My house has no trees near it.

• My house has flowers in the front yard.

• My house has windows with curtains.

• My neighbors to my left and my right have trees.

What Makes Sense?

Look at the numbers above each story. Use the numbers to fill in the blanks so that each story makes sense.

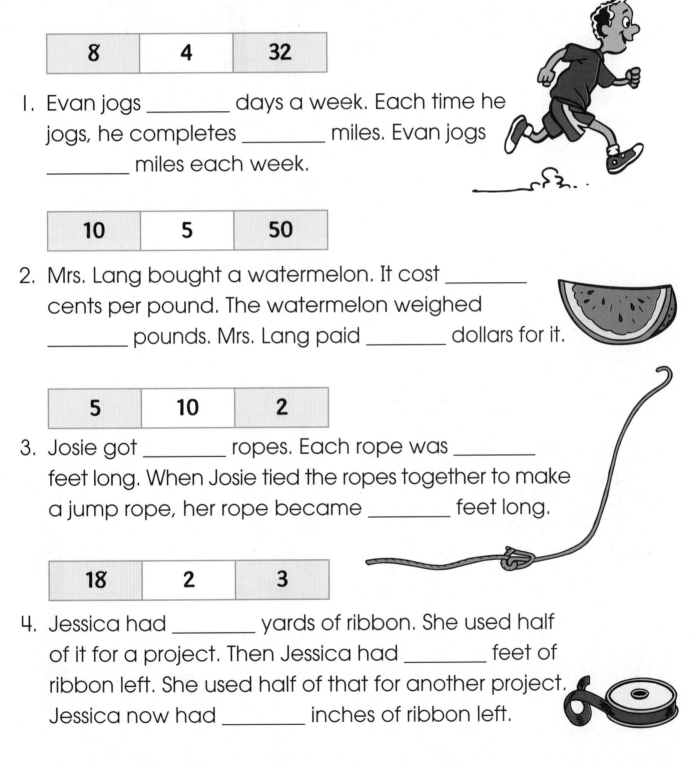

8	4	32

1. Evan jogs _____ days a week. Each time he jogs, he completes _____ miles. Evan jogs _____ miles each week.

10	5	50

2. Mrs. Lang bought a watermelon. It cost _____ cents per pound. The watermelon weighed _____ pounds. Mrs. Lang paid _____ dollars for it.

5	10	2

3. Josie got _____ ropes. Each rope was _____ feet long. When Josie tied the ropes together to make a jump rope, her rope became _____ feet long.

18	2	3

4. Jessica had _____ yards of ribbon. She used half of it for a project. Then Jessica had _____ feet of ribbon left. She used half of that for another project. Jessica now had _____ inches of ribbon left.

A Temperature Experiment

Name _____

Mr. Bowen's class did a science experiment. They wanted to find out how the air temperature changed during the day.

1. The students placed a thermometer outside. They recorded the temperature at 9:00. The students checked the temperature every half-hour after that. Their last temperature reading was at 2:30. How many times did they record the temperature?

   _____

   List the times of the temperature readings below.

   _____

   _____

   _____

2. From 9:00 to 1:00, the temperature rose by two degrees every half-hour. The temperature at 9:00 was 68° F.

   What was the temperature at 1:00? _____

3. From 1:00 to 2:30, the temperature dropped by three degrees every half-hour.

   What was the temperature at 2:30? _____

4. What was the highest temperature reading that day?

   _____

Work Backwards

Read these problems. Then try working backwards to get the answer!

1. Mrs. Wilson has invited some friends over for coffee and cake. They will arrive at 3:00 in the afternoon. Mrs. Wilson wants to bake the cake before they come. It will take 20 minutes to get the cake batter ready. Then the cake must bake for 1 hour and 15 minutes. Afterwards, it will need to cool for half an hour before it can be served. The cake must be ready by 3:00.

What is the latest time Mrs. Wilson can begin making her cake?

_____

2. Mr. Campbell is going on a business trip. He wants to be back home for his son's birthday party on June 2. Mr. Campbell plans to arrive home the day before the party. His trip will last five days, including the day he leaves and the day he comes back.

On what day is Mr. Campbell leaving for his trip?

_____

Anna's Slumber Party

Read the clues to find out when Anna is going to have her slumber party. On the calendar, place an **X** on all the days you know she cannot have the party. The remaining day is the day of Anna's party.

Clues:
- Anna has a science project due on the second Monday of the month. She will not have a party until the project is turned in.

- Anna will visit her grandparents on the third Friday of the month. She will stay with them over the weekend. She cannot have a party on those days.

- The party is not on an even-numbered day.

- Anna has to attend a wedding on the second Saturday of the month. She cannot have a party then.

- The day after the party is not a weekday.

Sun.	Mon.	Tues.	Wed.	Thurs.	Fri.	Sat.
	1	2	3	4	5	6
7	8	9	10	11	12	13
14	15	16	17	18	19	20
21	22	23	24	25	26	27
28	29	30				

Anna's party is on _____ .

A Hiking Trip

Jason Cooper and his parents are going hiking. Each person will carry two items from the list below.

water bottles — 5 pounds	flashlight — 1 pound
rope — 4 pounds	tent — 6 pounds
first aid kit — 3 pounds	bag of trail mix — 2 pounds

Mr. Cooper will carry twice as much weight as his son will. Mrs. Cooper will carry 4 pounds less than Mr. Cooper will. Jason will carry 1 pound less than Mrs. Cooper will.

Under each person's name, list the items he or she will carry. Each person must carry at least two items.

• Mr. Cooper

_____

_____

• Mrs. Cooper

_____

_____

• Jason

_____

_____

Balance the Weights

This scale shows a group of blocks balanced by a group of balls.

1. If the blocks weighed 4 grams each, how much would each ball weigh?

   _____

2. If the balls weighed 6 grams each, how much would each block weigh?

   _____

3. If the blocks weighed 12 grams each, how much would each ball weigh?

   _____

4. If the balls weighed 12 grams each, how much would each block weigh?

   _____

5. If one block was placed on the left side of the scale and one ball was placed on the right side of the scale, which way would the scale tip? Why?

   _____

   _____

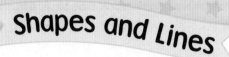

Shapes and Lines

1. Draw a square using four lines. (This should be easy!) Then draw two squares using just five lines!

2. Draw two squares using six lines.

3. Draw a triangle using three lines. Then try drawing two triangles using only four lines!

4. Draw two triangles using five lines.

Perimeter Problems

Perimeter is the distance around a figure or region. You find the perimeter by adding the lengths of the sides. For example, the rectangle at the right has a perimeter of 14 feet.

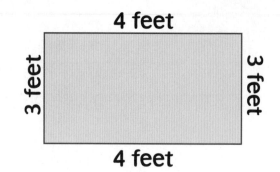

4 feet

3 feet

3 feet

4 feet

Solve the perimeter problems below.

1. Farmer Bill built a pen for his animals. The pen is in the shape of a rectangle. One side of the pen is 20 feet. The other side is half as long. What is the perimeter of the pen?

_____

2. Farmer Sal built a pen for her animals. The pen is in the shape of a square. The perimeter of the pen is 100 feet. What is the length of each side?

_____

3. Farmer Lou built two square-shaped pens side by side. One side of the first pen formed the side of the other pen. The perimeter of the joined pens is 54 feet. How long are the sides of each square?

_____

4. Farmer Joe and Farmer Bo each built a pen. The pens have the same perimeter. Farmer Joe's pen is in the shape of a triangle. Each side of the triangle is the same length. Farmer Bo's pen is in the shape of a hexagon. Each side of the hexagon is the same length.

If the pens have a perimeter of 60 feet, what is the length of each pen's side?

Farmer Joe's pen _____   Farmer Bo's pen _____

If the pens have a perimeter of 90 feet, what is the length of each pen's side?

Farmer Joe's pen _____   Farmer Bo's pen _____

If both pens have a perimeter of 120 feet, what is the length of each pen's side?

Farmer Joe's pen _____   Farmer Bo's pen _____

What do you know about the sides of Farmer Joe's pen compared to the sides of Farmer Bo's pen?

_____

_____

Cut the Pies

A baker wants to cut the pies below. Can you help him?
(The pieces of pie do not have to be the same shape or size.)

1. Draw two lines across the pie to make four pieces.

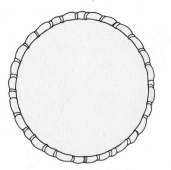

2. Draw two lines across the pie to make three pieces.

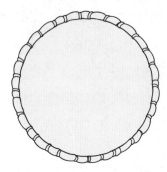

3. Draw three lines across the pie to make six pieces.

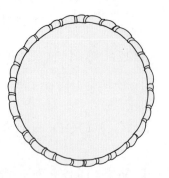

4. Draw three lines across the pie to make seven pieces.

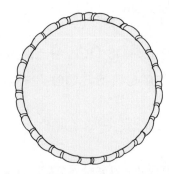

5. Draw four lines across the pie to make eight pieces.

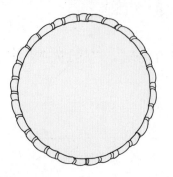

6. Draw four lines across the pie to make nine pieces.

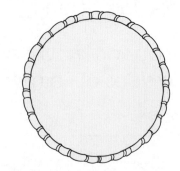

Pablo's Pictures

Pablo is a painter. He loves to create interesting pictures! Help him finish his pictures by following these directions.

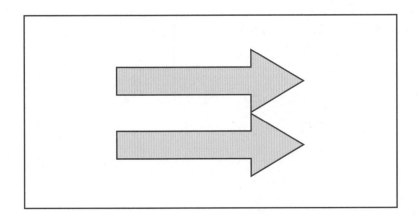

1. Add two lines to the picture to create a third arrow.

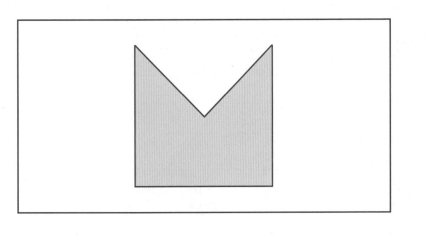

2. Add two lines to divide the shape into three equal parts.

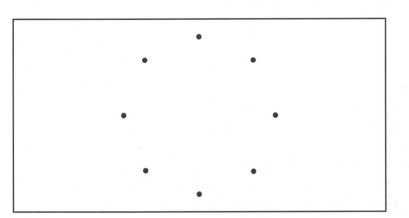

3. Connect the dots in such a way that you get two squares.

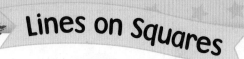
Name _____

You may want a pencil, a pair of scissors, and some paper squares to help you solve these problems!

1. Laura drew a line on a paper square. Then she cut the paper in half along its diagonal. This is what her pieces looked like.

   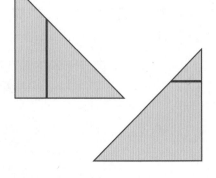

   What did the square look like before she cut it? Choose from the squares below. Circle your answer.

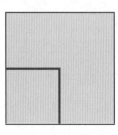 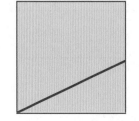 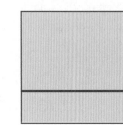 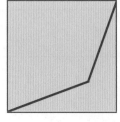

2. Peter drew a line on a paper square. Then he cut the paper in half along its diagonal. This is what his pieces looked like.

   What did the square look like before he cut it? Choose from the squares below. Circle your answer.

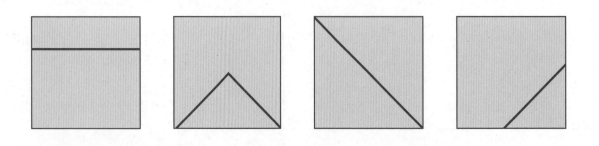

Matthew's Meals

Matthew is learning to cook. Every Friday, he makes dinner for his family. He always prepares the main course, one side dish, and a dessert. Here are the foods that Matthew has learned to make so far:

Main Course — spaghetti, meat loaf

Side Dish — peas, salad

Dessert — muffin, pudding

1. List all the possible food combinations that Matthew could make for dinner.

   _____   _____

   _____   _____

   _____   _____

   _____   _____

2. How many different combinations could Matthew make?

   _____

3. Suppose Matthew learned to make baked chicken for a main course. How many more combinations could he make?

   _____

Flora's Flower Shop

Flora has a flower shop. In her shop, she sells flowers in pots. Each pot has a pretty bow.

Flora has red, blue, and yellow flowers. She has red, blue, and yellow pots. Her bows are red, blue, and yellow as well. For each potted flower, Flora never uses a color more than once. For example, she doesn't put a red flower in a red pot with a red bow.

Color the flowers, pots, and bows to show the different combinations Flora can make.

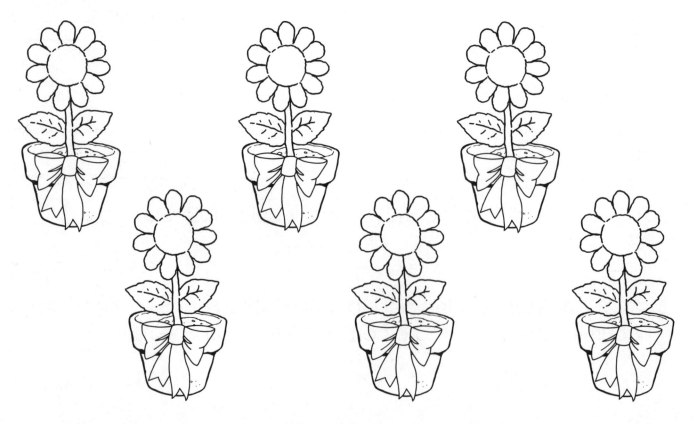

Color Spinners

Name _____

Kyle, Mark, Dan, and Nick made four different spinners for a game.

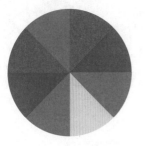
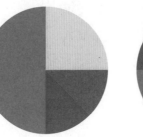
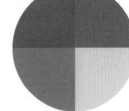
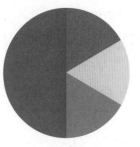

| Kyle | Mark | Dan | Nick |

The boys tested each spinner 16 times. The graphs show the results they got. Find the spinner that matches each graph. Write the boy who made that spinner on the line.

Suppose you wanted a spinner in which all four colors had an equal chance of being chosen. Whose spinner would you choose?

_____

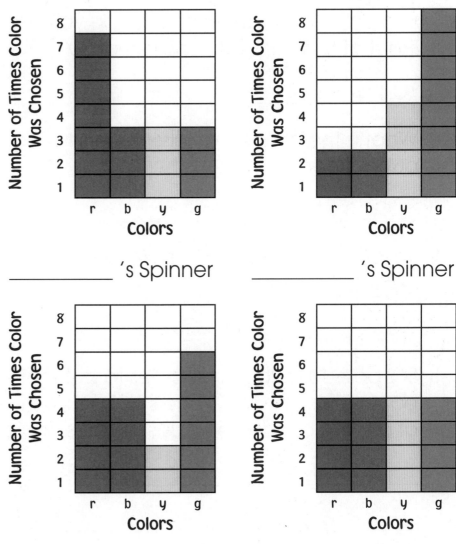

_____ 's Spinner

_____ 's Spinner

_____ 's Spinner

_____ 's Spinner

A Yummy Surprise

Miss Rogers is rewarding her class with a surprise—a bag of special treats! Inside the bag are 20 plastic eggs filled with candy. There are 5 yellow eggs, 5 light blue eggs, 5 dark blue eggs, and 5 green eggs.

1. Miss Rogers is going to take out one egg at a time and hand it to a student. What is the chance that the egg will be yellow— 1 out of 5, 5 out of 10, or 5 out of 20?

   _____

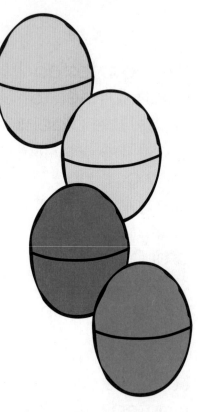

2. What is the chance of Miss Rogers taking out a green egg?

   _____

3. What is the chance of Miss Rogers taking out a blue egg?

   _____

4. Suppose Miss Rogers decides to put the eggs into two separate bags. What can Miss Rogers do so that she has the same chance of picking a green egg as she does of picking a blue egg?

   _____

   _____

   _____

Answer Key—Reading

Page 9
prickly
sturdy
silky
slender
lively
fatigued

Page 10
journey, expedition, voyage
final, end, ultimate
scrumptious, yummy, tasty
clean, tidy, orderly
terrify, scare, horrify

Page 11
Sydney's new speech will vary.

Make sure that children select their words from the Word List provided.

Page 12
dirty, clean
gentle, rough
rude, polite
dull
mean, kind

Page 13

Page 14
Pictures will vary.

Page 15
3   1   6
5   4   2

Page 16
A
B
B
A
A
B

Page 17
1. 3
2. 2
3. 4
4. 1
5. 4, 1, 3

Page 18
than
thorough
mere
through
then
mirror

Page 19
united
weather
know
untied
whether
now

Page 20
leave
tired
dull
dry
real

Page 21
bright
thick
heavy
serious
slow
strict

Page 22
numerous
celebrated
flock
vivid
transform
magnificent

Page 23
Students answers and pictures will vary.

Page 24
C, C, B

Page 26
Rorie is the main character.

Rorie had blond hair and was very pale.

1) She read everything she could find.

2) She carried books in her bag in case she had time to read.

"I would rather read."

Rorie's teacher told her mother that she was lucky to have a daughter like Rorie.

Page 27
Interview questions and answers will vary.

Page 28
Settings will vary.

Page 29
You would hear silverware clanking and lots of loud voices.

You would smell warm bread, boiling tomato sauce, and sweet chocolate cake.

You would see people coming and going at all hours.

Page 30
The story took place at night.

Tuesday

The family made mini-pizzas.

Page 31
The story took place in the winter.

It took place in Stratton, Vermont.

The story took place on the Fourth of July.

It took place in West Hartford, Connecticut.

It took place in the summer.

The story took place in space.

Page 32
Maps will vary.

Page 33
Travel brochures will vary.

Page 34
Answers will vary.

Page 35
Newspaper articles will vary.

Page 36
fiction

nonfiction

Page 37
8
5
1
X
2
3
X
7
X
6
4

Page 39
2
4
3
6
5
1

Page 41
C
B
A
A

Page 42
Writing in a diary can be helpful.

Leslie is good at many things.

Mr. Parson loves chocolate.

Page 43
C

Page 45

paintings

C

Some of the animals were deer, wild oxen, horses, and reindeer.

It meant that the hunter wished for survival and success on a hunt.

Page 46

California, Oregon, and Washington should be highlighted.

You should highlight words, phrases.

Page 48

Goose bumps are tiny bumps that appear on your arms when you are cold.

Highlight the following answers:

human bumps

the hairs stand up to try to trap more air and keep us warm

animals trap air and stay warmer

it fluffs out their feathers or fur

Page 49

A

You must practice for half an hour every day.

Page 50

Eddie knows a lot about computers.

1) He knows how to debug computers.

2) He knows how to write difficult programs.

Parents, teachers, and even the principal have called Eddie for computer help.

Page 51

They catch a lot of big fish.

Page 52

His mother didn't pack him any dessert.

The Boy Scouts take a lot of time to prepare to go camping in the winter.

Because they are so prepared, they always have a great time.

Page 53

They tape their tents to the boat with many layers of strong duct tape.

Some people prefer to sleep in a tent.

Page 55

Effect: Their grandparents were very happy to see them.

Cause: The car ride was very long and hot.

Effect: It made the back seat cooler.

Effect: She decided to take a picture.

Cause: It is disrespectful to walk inside the mausoleum with shoes on.

Cause: The sun was shining brightly.

Effect: Jyoti and Deepa started jumping and hopping on the hot marble floor.

Page 56

The Olympic skier was very athletic and loved challenges.

The English Knight was very well-mannered.

Drinking lots of coffee can prevent you from sleeping.

The comedian was silly and loved to make crazy faces.

The California Gold Rush in 1849 was an exciting time in history.

Running for President takes a lot of energy, hard work, and perseverance.

Page 57

B

Answers will vary.

Page 59

It is evening.

It is summer.

Christine's family stayed for the weekend.

There are probably 10 people because they boiled 20 ears of corn on the cob. We know that there is a total of two families.

Christine is polite and curious. (Answers will vary.)

Mrs. McMahon is kind and explains things. (Answers will vary.)

The cottage is called *Firelight Place* because of the flickering lights caused by the fireflies.

Page 60

The last straw is when a person is pushed to his or her limit and feels angry or frustrated.

Matt will change what he is doing and start fresh to make things different and better.

Page 61

Pictures of what will happen next will vary.

Page 62

He asked her if she would like to help him coach the younger soccer players.

Answers will vary.

Page 63

Carol likes to draw numbers in art class.

Carol's mom is proud of her daughter.

Carol's mom will ask the cashier to check the grocery slip.

Carol will be a mathematician when she grows up.

Page 64

B
A
B

Page 66

a bird that gets up at the quack of dawn

take away his credit cards

hard-boiled eggs

Answer Key—Writing

Page 67
person – man
place – library
thing – quarter

Page 68
Children should write the name of each noun on the lines provided.

Page 70
drives, dances, shoots, eats, discovers
Sentences will vary.

Page 71
tiny, lumpy, scary, spotted, Pink

Page 72
Summer is my favorite season.
My pet turtle eats a lot!
The cheetah runs fast.
A rose has thorns on its stem.
Blue is Kim's favorite color.

Page 73
Sentence endings will vary.

Page 74
Sentence beginnings will vary.

Page 75
First, Next, Last

Page 76
Pictures and sentences will vary. Make sure that children use the order words *first*, *next*, and *last* in their writing.

Page 77
Lists will vary.

Page 79
Herman, the Hulking Mouse/Strongest Mouse in the Universe!
The elephants are wearing tutus.
Herman is wearing a cape.
Herman is lifting two elephants.
A clown is sneaking up behind Herman.
The clown is tying Herman's shoelaces together.

Page 80
universe, elephants, tutus, cape, two, clown, tying

Page 82
Answers will vary but should be associated with sounds.

Page 83
Ideas will vary.

Page 85
Answers will vary.

Page 86
Ideas will vary.

Page 88
Answers will vary.

Page 89
Answers will vary.

Page 90
Stories will vary but should focus on setting.

Page 91
Paragraphs and pictures will vary.

Page 92
It is summer.
It is time for the sunset.

Page 93
Word lists will vary.

Page 94
Stories will vary.

Page 96
Story endings will vary.

Page 97
Story endings will vary.

Page 98
Story beginnings and middles will vary.

Page 99
Story beginnings and middles will vary.

Page 100
Ideas will vary.

Page 101
Stories will vary.

Page 102
Word lists will vary.

Page 103
Stories will vary.

Page 104
Story beginnings will vary.

Page 105
Story beginnings will vary.

Page 106
Story middles will vary.

Page 107
Story middles will vary.

Page 108
Story endings will vary.

Page 109
Story endings will vary.

Page 110
Ideas will vary.

Page 111
Stories will vary.

Page 112
Adjectives will vary.

Page 113
I wish I kud fli in a plane
two skule. i ride the buss. Howe old due yew think I am?

Pages 114 and 115
Stories and illustrations will vary.

Page 116
Answers will vary.

Page 117
Answers will vary.

Page 119
Letters will vary.

Page 120
Stories will vary.

Page 121
Stories and pictures will vary.

Page 122
Stories and pictures will vary.

Page 123
Stories will vary.

Pages 124 and 125
Stories will vary.

Page 127
The number of the Carneys' apartment is 98.

Page 128
1. 53
2. 761
3. 244
4. 525
5. 942
6. 407
7. 150
8. 73
9. 68
10. 375

Page 129
1. 1,467
2. 7,641
3. 4,167
4. 1,764
5. 6,471
6. 4,671
7. 7,614

Page 130
1. 27, 28, 32, 34
2. 65, 67, 71, 73
3. 85, 86, 89, 94

Page 131
1. 391, 394, 413, 419, 431, 439
2. 623, 625, 632, 635, 562, 563
3. 780, 782, 802, 807, 820, 827

Page 132

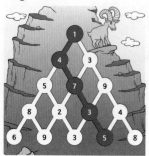

Page 133
1. The shortest route from Anytown to Elk Falls is 30 miles. The bus would go through Anytown, Bigville, and Elk Falls.
2. The shortest route is 44 miles.
   The longest route is 52 miles.
3. The towns that make up the shortest route are: Anytown, Bigville, Cityway, Dusty Roads, and Elk Falls.
4. The towns that make up the longest route are: Anytown, Cityway, Bigville, Dusty Roads, and Elk Falls.

Page 134
1.

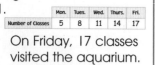

	Mon.	Tues.	Wed.	Thurs.	Fri.
Number of Classes	5	8	11	14	17

On Friday, 17 classes visited the aquarium.
2. (Your child may begin by guessing the number of starfish and octopuses, and determining the number of arms. Your child can then adjust his or her guess, depending on if the number of arms ends up being too high or too low.) There are 6 starfish and 5 octopuses.

Page 135

	Day 1	Day 2	Day 3	Day 4	Day 5	Day 6	Day 7
Sammy	15	30	45	60	75	90	105
Salty	25	50	75	100	125	150	175

Salty will have eaten 50 more pounds of fish than Sammy after 5 days.
Salty will have eaten 100 more pounds of fish than Sammy after 10 days.

	Day 8	Day 9	Day 10
Sammy	120	135	150
Salty	200	225	250

Page 136
1. 5 + 2 - 3 = 4
2. 6 + 5 - 4 = 7
3. 12 - 4 - 1 = 7
4. 10 - 9 + 8 = 9
5. 6 + 5 + 4 - 1 = 14
6. 12 - 2 - 10 + 8 = 8
7. 15 + 6 - 4 - 2 = 15
8. 8 - 3 + 6 + 10 = 21

Page 137
(Have your child begin by guessing an age, then checking it against the criteria presented in each problem.)
1. Kim is 10 years old, Kim's mom is 30 years old, and Kim's grandmother is 60 years old.
2. The boys' ages are 6, 7, 8, and 9.
3. Jenny is 12 years old, and Ann is 4 years old.

Page 138
1. The top shelf has 22 cans, the second shelf has 24 cans, the third shelf has 26 cans, and the bottom shelf has 28 cans.
2. There are 22 bottles of grape juice, 18 bottles of apple juice, and 12 bottles of cranberry juice.
3. Mrs. Kerr will have to buy 3 bags of beans.
   (Help your child see that since two servings for six people equals 12 servings, Mrs. Kerr will need to buy 3 bags - 2 bags would not be enough.)

Page 139
4. The line of boxes is 58 inches long.
5. Mr. Gorman has to buy 2 loaves of bread and 3 boxes of crackers.
6. There were 6 customers there at 5 o'clock.
   (Your child may try to solve this problem by working backwards:
   8 - 4 + 1 - 2 + 3 = 6)

Page 140

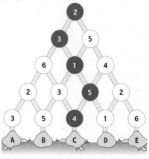

Page 141
1. 4 X 2 ÷ 1 = 8
2. 10 ÷ 5 X 3 = 6
3. 12 ÷ 3 X 4 = 16

4. $7 \times 4 \div 2 = 14$
5. $3 \times 4 \times 2 \div 6 = 4$
6. $3 \times 4 \div 2 \div 6 = 1$
7. $8 \div 2 \times 3 \div 4 = 3$
8. $15 \div 3 \times 2 \times 3 = 30$

Page 142
1. Barry has 13 cars.
2. Harry has 17 cars.
3. Larry has 19 cars.

Page 143
(Each row is formed by adding the digits in the preceding number to produce the next number.)
26 - 8
123 - 6
58 - 13 - 4
809 - 17 - 8
1,387 - 19 - 10 - 1

Answers will vary.

Page 144
1. 10
2. 5, 20
3. Numbers will vary.

Page 145
1.
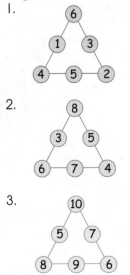

2.

3.

Page 146
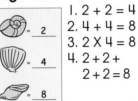
1. $2 + 2 = 4$
2. $4 + 4 = 8$
3. $2 \times 4 = 8$
4. $2 + 2 + 2 + 2 = 8$

Page 147
1. $1 + 1 = 2$
2. $1 + 2 = 3$
3. $1 \times 2 = 2$
4. $1 + 1 + 1 = 3$

Page 148
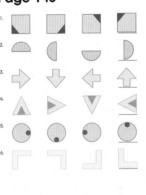

Page 149

4. The three numbers forming the points of each triangle are even numbers.

Page 150
1. The coins should be filled in as follows: 2 dimes, 4 nickels. Jessica has 40¢.
2. The coins should be filled in as follows: 2 quarters, 3 dimes, 1 penny. Sarah has 81¢ altogether.
3. Scott has 1 half dollar, 1 dime, and 2 nickels. Vicky has 2 quarters and 2 dimes.
4. Amy has 1 quarter and 1 nickel, so she has 30¢. Wendy has 3 dimes; she also has 30¢.

Page 151

Week	Jan Amount Saved for the Week	Jan Total Amount Saved
1	$1.25	$1.25
2	$1.25	$2.50
3	$1.25	$3.75
4	$1.25	$5.00
5	$1.25	$6.25
6	$1.25	$7.50
7	$1.25	$8.75
8	$1.25	$10.00

Week	Fran Amount Saved for the Week	Fran Total Amount Saved
1	$.50	$.50
2	$1.00	$1.50
3	$1.50	$3.00
4	$2.00	$5.00
5	$2.50	$7.50
6	$3.00	$10.50
7	$3.50	$14.00
8	$4.00	$18.00

Fran will save $10.00 first.

Page 152
1. The captain collected $70.00 (10 X $4.00 and 10 X $3.00)
2. There were 8 adults and 12 children on the boat. (8 X $4.00 and 12 X $3.00)
3. The most amount of money the captain could collect would be $79.00 (19 X $4.00 and 1 X $3.00)
4. The least amount of money the captain could collect would be $61.00. (1 X $4.00 and 19 X $3.00)

Page 153
Mrs. Rogers bought 24 cookies.
Mr. Grant bought 12 cookies.
Miss Lang bought 6 cookies.
(Your child can try working backwards to solve this problem. Start with Mrs. Soo's 6 cookies. Multiply the 6 by 2 to get the number of cookies available to Miss Lang(12). She bought 6. Multiply that by 2 to get the number available when Mr. Grant purchased his cookies (12), and so on. 48 cookies were for sale when the bakery first opened.

Page 154
1. 12 of the circles should be colored blue, 6 of the circles should be colored yellow, and 6 of the circles should be colored red.
2. Three-fourths (3/4)
3. One-half (1/2)
4. Three-fourths (3/4)

Page 155

	Solid-Colored	Speckled	Striped	Total Number of Rocks
Week 1	4	2	2	8
Week 2	8	4	4	16
Week 3	12	6	6	24
Week 4	16	8	8	32

1. The numbers increase by 8.
2. The numbers increase by 4.
3. The numbers increase by 2.
4. Jeff will find a total of 40 rocks in Week 5.

Page 156

1. 7/18
2. 2/3
3. 6/18 or 1/3
4. 3/4
5. 9/18 or 1/2

Sentences will vary.

Page 157

Trevor's Clues: • Blue is next to green.
• Red is next to blue.
• Red is at the top.
• Yellow is between green and brown.

Margo's Clues: • Orange is between red and blue.
• Red is between orange and yellow.
• Purple is next to yellow.
• Blue is not at the bottom.

Page 158

Child	Dog	Prize
Mandy	collie	first
Randy	beagle	second
Sandy	poodle	third

(Have your child read the clues and fill in what he or she knows for sure. For example, for Randy, your child can write "second" under the Prize heading. Then let your child use the process of elimination to complete the chart. For example, since Sandy's dog did not win first prize, it must have won third.)

Page 159

Child	Age	Ice Cream
Lana	8	chocolate
Lori	9	strawberry
Lily	10	vanilla

Page 160

1. 3 apples
   3 oranges
   4 pears
   2 bananas
2. 2 apples
   4 oranges
   5 pears
   1 banana
3. 6 apples
   3 oranges
   2 pears
   1 banana

Page 161

Hop-Along will not land on a lily pad more than once. He can hop from one lily pad to another only if they are connected. Color the path that will give Hop-Along the greatest sum!

For an extra challenge, use a different color of crayon to color a path that will give Hop-Along the least sum!

Numbers 1, 2, 3, 6, 9, and 12 should be colored to show the path that will give Hop-Along the least sum.

Page 162

1. star = 4
   heart = 2
   diamond = 6
2. triangle = 7
   circle = 4
   spade = 5

Page 163

1. 54
2. 325
3. 431
4. 116
5. The symbol stands for the number of ones.
6. The symbol stands for the number of tens.
7. The symbol stands for the number of hundreds.

Answers will vary.

Page 164

1. 27
   (One strategy is to use craft sticks to represent the students. The sticks can be lined up and labeled. For example, the seventh stick can be labeled "T" for Tina. Six sticks can be placed after the "T" stick, and then the next stick laid down can be labeled "K" for Kristy.)
2. There are 12 rows of seats on the bus. (A diagram can be made to represent the rows:

		K					T				
)

3. 8 students are standing between Tina and Jeffrey.

Page 165

(Your child may want to draw 30 circles to represent the children in line. Your child can then mark off the appropriate number of circles indicating every seventh child, every fourth child, and so on.)
1. 4
2. 7
3. 1
4. 2

Page 166

The second house in the second row should be circled.

Page 167

1. 4, 8, 32
2. 50, 10, 5
3. 2, 5, 10
4. 2, 3, 18

Page 168

1. The students recorded the temperature 12 times.
   9:00 10:30 12:00 1:30
   9:30 11:00 12:30 2:00
   10:00 11:30 1:00 2:30
2. 84°F
3. 75°F
4. 84°F

Page 169

1. 12:55
   (3:00 subtract half
   an hour - 2:30
   2:30 subtract 1 hour
   and 15 minutes - 1:15
   1:15 subtract 20
   minutes - 12:55)
2. May 28

June 2	June 1	May 31	May 30	May 29	May 28
day of party	arrive home				leave for trip

5 days

Page 170

Anna's party is on the 27th.

Page 171

Mr. Cooper will carry
the tent and the rope.
(6 pounds plus 4
pounds)
Mrs. Cooper will carry
the water bottles and
the flashlight. (5
pounds plus 1 pound)
Jason will carry the first
aid kit and the bag of
trail mix. (3 pounds plus
2 pounds)

Page 172

1. 3 grams (blocks - 3 X
   4 = 12 grams; balls -
   4 X 3 grams = 12
   grams)
2. 8 grams (balls - 4 X 6
   grams = 24 grams;
   blocks - 3 X 8 grams
   = 24 grams)
3. 9 grams (blocks - 3 X
   12 grams = 36 grams;
   balls - 4 X 9 grams =
   36 grams)
4. 16 grams (balls - 4 X
   12 grams = 48 grams;
   blocks - 3 X 16 = 48
   grams)

5. The scale would tip
   to the left (towards
   the block), because
   one block is heavier
   than one ball.

Page 173

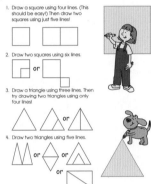

Page 174

1. 60 feet (20 feet + 20
   feet + 10 feet + 10
   feet)
2. 25 feet
3. 9 feet

Page 175

4. If the perimeter is 60
   feet, Farmer Joe's
   pen is 20 feet per
   side; Farmer Bo's
   is 10 feet.
   If the perimeter is 90
   feet, Farmer Joe's
   pen is 30 feet per
   side; Farmer Bo's
   is 15 feet.
   If the perimeter is 120
   feet, Farmer Joe's
   pen is 40 feet per
   side; Farmer Bo's
   is 20 feet.

   The sides of Farmer
   Joe's pen are twice
   as long as the sides

of Farmer Bo's pen.

Page 176

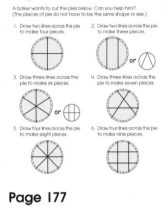

Page 177

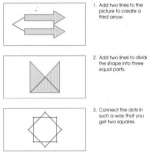

Page 178

1. The second shape
   should be circled.
2. The fourth shape
   should be circled.
   (Your child may
   want to get some
   paper squares and
   copy the possible
   solutions. When your
   child cuts the
   squares along their
   diagonals, the
   correct answers will
   become clear.)

Page 179

1. spaghetti, peas, muffin
   spaghetti, peas, pudding
   spaghetti, salad, muffin
   spaghetti, salad, pudding
2. There are 8 possible

combinations.
meat loaf, peas, muffin
meat loaf, peas, pudding
meat loaf, salad, muffin
meat loaf, salad, pudding

3. If Matthew made
   chicken for the main
   course, he could make
   4 more combinations:
   chicken, peas, muffin
   chicken, peas, pudding
   chicken, salad, muffin
   chicken, salad, pudding

Page 180

Page 181

Nick's   Mark's
Spinner   Spinner

Kyle's   Dan's
Spinner   Spinner

You would choose
Dan's spinner if you
wanted a spinner in
which all four colors
had an equal chance
of being chosen.

Page 182

1. 5 out of 20
2. 5 out of 20 (or 1 out of 4)
3. 10 out of 20 (or 1 out of 2)
4. Miss Rogers can put
   5 green eggs and 5
   blue eggs in one
   bag. She can put
   the remaining eggs
   in the second bag.